AF255209

BIBLICAL TOPOGRAPHY.

BIBLICAL TOPOGRAPHY.

BY

REV. GEORGE RAWLINSON, M.A.

CANON RESIDENTIARY OF CANTERBURY, AND
CAMDEN PROFESSOR OF ANCIENT HISTORY IN THE
UNIVERSITY OF OXFORD.

WIPF & STOCK · Eugene, Oregon

Wipf and Stock Publishers
199 W 8th Ave, Suite 3
Eugene, OR 97401

Biblical Topography
By Rawlinson, George
Softcover ISBN-13: 978-1-6667-8035-2
Hardcover ISBN-13: 978-1-6667-8036-9
eBook ISBN-13: 978-1-6667-8037-6
Publication date 5/16/2023
Previously published by James Nisbet & Co., 1887

This edition is a scanned facsimile of the original edition published in 1887.

TABLE OF CONTENTS.

I.

THE SITE OF PARADISE . . . . . . PAGE I

Great variety of opinion on the point—A real locality intended—Geographical indications of the text of Genesis
—The Euphrates—The Tigris—Assyria—Arguments
against placing Paradise in Armenia—Arguments for
placing it in some part of the Mesopotamian plain—
Arguments against the present lower plain—Conclusion
that it was in the middle plain, between lat. 33° 30′ and
lat. 31°.

II.

THE EARLY CITIES OF BABYLONIA 20

Description of Babylonia—Its early condition—Its natural
productions—Babylonian cities mentioned in Genesis—
Identification of the site of Babylon—of Eresh—Doubtful
identification of Accad with Agadé, and of Caluch with
Niffer—Site of Ur, not Orfah, but Mugheir—Chief features of all these sites—Probable condition and habits
of the earliest occupants of Babylonia—Character of the
earliest cities—Early canals—Peculiar position of Ur—
Independence of the several cities.

III.

PAGE

THE CHIEF CITIES OF ANCIENT ASSYRIA . . . 41

Number of the cities mentioned in Genesis probably three
—Nineveh, Calah, Resen—Site of Nineveh described—
Supposed larger Nineveh—Character of the country about
Nineveh—Its rivers, the Tigris and the Khosr-Su—Site
of Calah—Description of the ruins—Site of Resen doubtful—General character of the Assyrian cities—Wall ornamentation—Emplacement on artificial mounds—Walls of
cities—Vegetable productions—Houses of the people—
—Fauna.

IV.

ELAM, ITS CHIEF CITY AND ITS CHIEF RIVER . . 61

First mention of Elam in Scripture—Expedition of Chedorlaomer—Elam the modern Khuzistan—Description of it
—The Plain—The mountains—Chief Elamitic rivers—
Situation of the capital, Susa—Its existing ruins—Antiquity of Susa—View from the Palace mound—Ancient
fauna of the neighbourhood—Susa under the Persians
—Special river of Susa—Ancient course of the Eulæus.

V.

SITES CONNECTED WITH ABRAHAM— HARRAN, DAMAS-
CUS, HEBRON 81

Haran of Genesis the modern Harran—Position of Harran
—Short stay of Abraham at the place—Abraham's sojourn at Damascus probably a fact—Description of the
site of Damascus—Beauties of the place would not tempt
Abraham to settle there—His start for Palestine—His
wanderings there—Hebron—Description of the site—
Sepulchral quadrangle there—Its external appearance—
Arrangement of the interior—Six of the seven tombs
genuine.

VI.

PAGE

Egyptian Sites—Zoan and Pithom 103

Chief Scriptural notices of Zoan—Its antiquity—Probably
the capital city of the Pharaoh of the Exodus—Scriptural
indications of its site—Indications met by the position of
Zan or San—Description of San as it is—Description of
Zan as it was—The "field of Zan or Zoan"—Its general
monotony—Pithom—Its claim to be a "treasure-city"
contested—Its situation, according to Herodotus—Its
identification with Tel-el-Maskoutah certain—Description
of its present condition—Site compared with that of
Zoan—Present and former appearance—Brings before us
the reality of the Israelite oppression.

VII.

Further Egyptian Sites—Memphis, Thebes, Migdol, Syene 124

Memphis—Its name and situation—Natural features of the
site—Scantiness of the ruins—The Necropolis of Memphis—Thebes—Its various names—Advantages of the
situation—Description of the remains of the city—Thebes
ruined by the Assyrians—Disappearance of the walls and
gates—Migdol—Several places of the name—Site of the
most famous Migdol—Syene—Its situation and quarries
—Beauty of the neighbourhood—Elephantine—The First
Cataract—Philæ.

BIBLICAL TOPOGRAPHY.

I.

THE SITE OF PARADISE.

THE learned Dr. Kalisch, in his Commentary upon Genesis, when approaching this subject, remarks that " scarcely any part of the habitable globe has remained without the honour of being regarded as the happy abode of our first parents." [1] The statement is an exaggeration, but it has a basis of fact to rest upon ; and if we substitute for " any part of the habitable globe" the words "any portion of south-western Asia or north-eastern Africa," there will not be much reason to find fault with it. The Garden of Eden, or Paradise, wherein our first parents dwelt, has been placed in

[1] " Historical and Critical Commentary on the Old Testament," vol. i. p. 67, E. T.

A

Armenia by Reland, Brugsch, Keil, Kurtz, and Baron Bunsen ; in the region immediately west of the Caspian Sea by Gesenius, Rosenmüller, and Tuch ; in Media Rhagiana by Von Bohlen ; on the Pamir plateau by Lenormant ; in Babylonia by Calvin, Pressel, Rask, Sir Henry Rawlinson, G. Smith, Professor Sayce, and Professor Delitzsch ; near Damascus by Le Clerc; in Palestine by Heidegger and Lakemacher; in southern Arabia by Herbin, Hardouin, and Halevy ; and on the upper Nile by Champollion. Nor does the variety of geographical location at all fully represent the diversity of views which have been held upon the subject. The Garden of Eden, according to some, is to be found only in Utopia, among the other pleasant fictions with which the prolific imagination of man beguiled and amused his childhood. Such was the teaching of Philo ; such, we are told, was the teaching of Origen ; such, so far as the Eden of Genesis is concerned, would seem to be the teaching of M. François Lenormant.[1] These writers relegate to mythology the prob-

---

[1] *Origines de l'histoire d'àpres la Bible,* vol. ii. p. 142.

lem which has so long puzzled geographers, and account for the diversity of geographical explanations on the ground that to attempt a geographical explanation is a mistake, and that no satisfactory one is possible.

To us it appears that a geographic character manifestly attaches to the entire description contained in the second chapter of Genesis, and that it would be contrary to all sound canons of historical or literary criticism to treat as mythic or allegorical a passage of a narrative, the general historical character of which is allowed, when there is nothing in the passage itself suggestive of either myth or allegory. Now the narrative is markedly matter of fact. It professes to describe the position of the original home of the human race ; and it describes this position by a number of geographic names, most of which occur elsewhere in Biblical geography, by a reference to the points of the compass, and by an enumeration of the valuable commodities which one of the countries mentioned produces. Dr. Kalisch says with reason : " Eden is geographically described in a manner which leaves no doubt that a distinct locality was before the mind of the author."[1] The real point for consideration is, What was that locality ? Theories of a Utopian or imaginary Eden, without earthly location, may be pronounced out of court.

In attempting to determine among the various geographic theories which is the more probable, we must be guided mainly, if not solely, by the words of the narrative. It is necessary therefore, in the first instance, to reproduce as nearly as possible the original words. They are as follow :

" The Lord God (*Jehovah Elohim*) planted a garden eastward in Eden, and there He placed the man whom He had formed. . . . And a river went out of Eden to water the garden, and from thence it was parted (or, it parted itself), and became into four heads. The name of the first is Pishon ; that is it which compasseth the whole land of Havilah, where there is gold, and the gold of that land is good ; there is *bedolah*, and the *shoham* stone. And the name of the second river is Gihon

---

[1] " Commentary," vol. i. p. 74.

(Gikhon) ; that is it which compasseth the whole land of Cush. And the name of the third river is Hiddekel ; that is it which floweth before Assyria. And the fourth river, that is Pĕrâth " (Euphrates, A.V.)

Now we have here, in the limited space of seven verses, eight geographic names. Four of them are names of rivers—Pishon, Gihon, Hiddekel, and Pĕrâth ; four of them, Eden, Havilah, Cush, and Assyria (Asshur), names of countries. Let us inquire how many of these can be certainly identified. And first, of the rivers.

It is almost universally allowed that the fourth river—the Pĕrâth—is the Euphrates. The name of the Euphrates in the Assyrian cuneiform inscriptions is *Purât* or *Purâta ;* in the Persian cuneiform it is *Ufratush,* whence the Greek Εὐφράτης ; in the Arabic it is Furat or F'rât. The Hebrew Pĕrâth is closer to the original Assyrian than any of the other representatives. In the Old Testament it occurs nineteen times, and is uniformly translated Εὐφράτης by the Septuagint interpreters. The word means, in Assyrian, " the stream," or

" the great stream "[1]—and the Hebrew designation of it as " the river " (*nahar, han-nahar*), or " the great river " (*han-nahar haggadol*), is in close accordance with the etymology. (See Gen. xv. 8 ; Ex. xxiii. 31 ; Isa. vi. 20, viii. 7 ; Mic. vii. 12.)

The third river—the Hiddekel—is generally allowed to be the Tigris. In the cuneiform inscriptions of Assyria and Babylonia the name given to the Tigris is either *Idiklat* or *Diklat*. This became in the Syriac *Deklat*, in the Hebrew of the Targums and the Talmud *Diglâth*, in Arabic *Digla*, in Pehlevi *Digrath*, in the Persian cuneiform *Tigrâ*, and in Greek and Latin *Tigris*. Of the classical writers Pliny alone has preserved a form nearer to the original and native appellation, viz., *Diglito* (Hist. Nat. vi. 27). The Hebrew " Hiddekel " is peculiarly close to the most ancient and fullest form of the word, which is *I-diglat*, or *Idiklat*. This is thought to mean,

---

[1] See Delitzsch, *Wo lag das Paradies?* (Appendix I. p. 169). *Pur pura*, in Akkadian, means "the deep," "a river bed," "a river." *Purât* is nothing but this word with the ordinary Semitic feminine suffix attached to it.

"the stream with high banks"[1]—a very appropriate name for the Tigris, especially if it is compared with the Euphrates. "Hiddekel" occurs only twice in the Old Testament (Gen. ii. 14; Dan. x. 4). In neither place have the Septuagint interpreters ventured to translate it; but few commentators have been able to resist the evidence furnished by the name itself, backed up as it is by the connection with Assyria (Gen. ii. 14), and by Daniel's visiting it (Dan. *l.c.*); and the result has been that the third river is identified with nearly, though not quite, the same degree of certainty as the fourth.

Of the countries, one only is undoubted. As Asshur is the only name given to Assyria in the Old Testament, and as it occurs above a hundred times, and is almost uniformly rendered by the LXX. Ἀσσυρία or οἱ Ἀσσύριοι, no one has been as yet found hardy enough to question that Assyria is intended by "Asshur" in Gen. ii. 14.

To all the other geographic names under consideration more or less of doubt attaches;

---

[1] See Delitzsch, *Wo lag das Paradies?* (Appendix I. p. 171).

but the three identifications here laid down, which we regard as moral certainties, will enable us to dispose of a large number of the theories mentioned at the beginning of this paper. Eden cannot have been the region immediately to the west of the Caspian, or Media Rhagiana, or the Pamir plateau, or the tract about Damascus, or any part of Palestine, or a district of southern Arabia, or any portion of the Nile valley, since these are, all of them, regions remote from Assyria, and since no one of them borders either on the Tigris or on the Euphrates. The site of the "garden" must be sought somewhere along the courses of the two great streams of Western Asia, so plainly mentioned in Gen. ii. 13, and should not be very far distant from that portion of the Tigris which "floweth before Assyria."

The theory that the garden of Eden was in the heart of Armenia, the high mountain ranges about the sources of the Tigris and Euphrates, has in its favour a large number of important names, but seems to us open to insuperable objections. The tract is in winter a bitterly cold region, and the winter lasts six months of the year ; whereas the whole history of the paradisiacal state seems to us to imply that the garden was situated in the warmer portion of the temperate zone, not far outside the tropic. The single stream branching into four heads is not to be found in Armenia, where the sources even of the Tigris and the Euphrates lie at a considerable distance the one from the other. No Armenian Pishon can be found, for the Phasis is not an Armenian river ; and if the Araxes is pressed into service, to stand for the Gihon, since the Arabic geographers call it *Gaihun er-Ras*, it may be remarked that the sources of the Araxes are remote from those of both the Euphrates and the Tigris, and that with neither of these rivers has it any connection at all. Moreover, the other geographic names, Cush, Havilah, Eden, have no Armenian representatives, the resemblance of Havilah to Colchis, which some have urged, being at any rate not very apparent.

We must leave the mountains, and descend the courses of the streams to the great fertile plain which they water below the 34th parallel, before we come to a region at all suited for the habitation of primitive man—to a region which is naturally " a garden," and which in antiquity excited universal admiration. Here begins " the land of Shinar;" the region known to the Greeks and Romans as " Babylonia;" the region of which Herodotus says : " Of all the countries which we know there is none so fruitful in grain. It makes no pretension indeed of growing the fig, the olive, or the vine (?), or any other tree of the kind ; but in grain it is so fruitful as to yield commonly two hundred-fold, and when the production is the greatest even three hundred-fold. The blade of the wheat plant and barley plant is often four fingers in breadth. As for the millet and the sesame, I shall not say to what height they grow, though within my own knowledge ; for I am not ignorant that what I have already written concerning the fruitfulness of Babylonia must seem incredible to those who have never visited the region. . . . Palm-trees grow in great numbers over the whole of the flat country" (Book i. ch. 195). Theophrastus,

the disciple of Aristotle, writes : " In Babylonia, the wheat-fields are regularly mown
twice, and then fed off with beasts, to keep
down the luxuriance of the leaf; otherwise
the plant does not run to ear. When this
is done, the return, in lands that are badly
cultivated, is fifty-fold, while in those that are
well-farmed, it is a hundred-fold " (*Hist.
Plant.* viii. 7). The historians of Julian
declare that in his time, a forest of verdure
extended from the upper edge of the alluvium,
which he crossed, to Mesene, and the shores
of the Persian Gulf (Amm. Marc. xxiv. 3).
Zosimus says, that not only were the palm
groves continuous, but that the trees were
everywhere encircled by vines, which hung
about them in festoons, and sometimes climbed
to their tops, and thence depended with rich
clusters of grapes (Book iii. pp. 173–9). Even
in modern times " a thick forest of luxuriant
date-trees clothes the banks of the Euphrates
from the vicinity of Mugheir to its embouchure
at the head of the Persian Gulf." [1]

Before proceeding further, let us inquire

[1] " Ancient Monarchies," vol. i. pp. 35, 36.

whether the other geographic names connected with the garden of Eden in Genesis harmonise or conflict with the theory that places it in Babylonia. These names are five—Eden, Havilah, Cush, Gihon, and Pison.

The name of Eden appears in Scripture under a slightly modified form in 2 Kings xix. 12, and in Amos i. 5—in the latter passage designating a place, in the former a people. The Beth-Eden of Amos is either a city or a district, and being mentioned in connection with Damascus, should not be far from that locality. The Beni-Eden of the Second Book of Kings are a nation subdued by Assyria, and have been probably identified with the people of a region conquered by Asshur-izir-pal, and called Bīt-Adini, which seems to have been on the Middle Euphrates, not far from Circesium. Neither of these notices, consequently, can be said to be in close harmony with the theory which places Paradise in Babylonia. It has been suggested, however, that the original geographic use of the term *Eden* or *Edin* was a wide and vague one, that it signified "a plain," "a depression,"[1] and that hence it may have been applied to the Mesopotamian plain generally, within which the people of Beth-Adini seems to have dwelt. Again, it is thought that there may be a trace of the word Eden in an ancient name of Babylon, Kardunyas, *kar* being a dialectic form of *gan*, "garden," and *dunyas* a corruption of Eden.[2] Still, we must admit these speculations are uncertain, and that the name Eden does not greatly help the theory which places Paradise in Babylonia.

It is otherwise with the words Havilah and Cush. Havilah, which means "the sand region" (*Dünenland*),[3] is connected by the genealogy of Cush, and again by that of Joktan (Gen. x. 7, 29), with Arabia, and may well have been a name applied generally to the sandy tract which stretches from the Lower Euphrates to the mountains of Edom (Gen. xxv. 18), between the 30th and the 34th parallels. Havilah, in this case, would

---

[1] Delitzsch, *Wo lag das Paradies?* p. 80. The views expressed by this writer are criticised by M. Lenormant (*Origines de l'histoire*, vol. ii. pp. 530, 531).

[2] See the last cited work, p. 554.

[3] Delitzsch, *Wo lag das Paradies?* p. 12.

have skirted Babylonia along the whole of its western border; and if any stream branched from the Euphrates on this side, it might well be said to have been "compassed" by it. The three products for which Havilah was remarkable were anciently to be found in this country. Ophir was the main gold region of the early times; and Ophir adjoined upon Havilah (Gen. x. 29). *Bedôlah* is probably bdellium, as translated in the Authorised Version, and bdellium is "the gum of a tree growing in *Arabia*, India, and Babylon."[1] The *shoham*, or onyx, is also an Arabian gem, and was probably obtained from Arabia when needed for the breastplate of the high priest (Ex. xxviii. 9, 20; xxxix. 6, 13).

Cush, which so many critics have connected with Ethiopia, and placed upon the Middle Nile, designates, probably, in Gen. ii. 13, the tract on the eastern side of the Lower Tigris. Cush is coupled with Elam by Isaiah (xi. 11), and with Persia by Ezekiel (xxxviii. 5). Herodotus calls the Elam of Scripture Κισσία, and Diodorus Siculus places in this quarter

---

[1] Kalisch, "Commentary on Genesis," p. 74.

the Cossæans (xix. 19) ; in which terms many of the best etymologists have recognised the Hebrew *Kush* and the Akkadian *Kassi.* Eastern as well as western, Asiatic as well as African, Ethiopians are recognised both by Homer (*Od.* i. 23, 24) and Herodotus (iii. 94 ; vii. 70) ; and the land of Kush watered by the Pison is almost certainly the Eastern Cush, or the country still known as *Khuzi-stan.*

The names of Pison and Gihon still remain to be considered. Neither of these two names occurs elsewhere in Scripture. Neither has any clear or manifest representative in later geography, Assyrian, classical, or Arabian. A single writer thinks that he has found a name resembling Gihon attached to one of the great canals, or branch streams, which were anciently derived from the Euphrates ;[1] but his reading is questioned by a critic of equal eminence,[2] and the point must be regarded as one which still remains in dispute. The name Pison or Pishon has certainly not been found

---

[1] Delitzsch, p. 75.
[2] Lenormant, *Origines de l'histoire,* vol. ii. p. 536.

as that of any stream or canal, either in Babylonia or elsewhere, and remains up to the present date an inscrutable puzzle.

Still, on the whole, it must be said that the geographic names connected with those of the Tigris and Euphrates in Gen. ii. 10–14, so far as they support any theory at all, tend to strengthen the view that the site of the Garden was some portion of the alluvial plain through which the two great Mesopotamian rivers reach the sea.

Can we go further, and say in what portion of the plain it was probably situated? Here two theories, and two theories only, meet us. One places the Garden on the Shat-el-Arab, and finds the Pison and the Gihon in the Susianian rivers, which here mingle their waters with those of the two main streams. But it is conclusive against this view that the whole course of the Shat-el-Arab is of recent formation, the Persian Gulf having anciently reached 150 or 200 miles further inland than it does at present.[1] And it is also conclusive

---

[1] See Mr. C. H. H. Wright's article on "The Site of Paradise" in the *Nineteenth Century* for October 1882, p. 561.

against it that the Susianian streams are not branch streams from either the Euphrates or the Tigris, but simple tributaries of the latter, flowing into it from the Bakhtiyari mountains. In ancient times, moreover, it is most probable that they were not even connected with the Tigris, but reached the gulf by separate mouths.

The other theory, that of Calvin, Rask, Sir Henry Rawlinson, Mr. George Smith, Professor Sayce, and Professor Delitzsch, assigns for the site of the Garden the upper portion of the alluvium, or the rich and fertile tract extending along the courses of the two great rivers from about lat. 33° 30′ to lat. 31°. This is the region described in such glowing terms by Herodotus and Theophrastus, by Zosimus and Ammianus Marcellinus. It is a region where streams abound, where they divide and re-unite, where alone in the Mesopotamian tract can be found the phenomenon of a single river parting itself into four arms, each of which is, or has been, a river of consequence. The Euphrates above Felujiyeh flows at a higher level than the Tigris, and about lat. 33° 23′

throws off an arm which reaches the Tigris at
Baghdad, and sometimes threatens that city
with destruction.[1] Lower down it throws off
a second arm to the west, which, passing by
Kerbela and the Birs-i-Nimrud, flows into
the Bahr-i-Nedjif, and thence pursues a south-
eastern course, skirting the Arabian desert by
Tel-el-Lahm, Abu-Shahrein, and Zobair, to
the Persian Gulf, which it enters in lat. 30°.
This branch was known to the Greeks as the
Pallacopas, and, having been improved and
straightened by human art, was reckoned as
a canal. In the Biblical narrative it seems to
be called "the Pison." The Tigris, largely
increased by the waters poured into it from
the Euphrates,[2] divides at Kut-el-Amarah, and
forms two streams of almost equal size, either
of which may be regarded as the main river.
The author of Gen. ii. regarded the western
arm (now the Shat-el-Hie) as the true " Hiddekel "—the continuation of the stream which
had " flowed before Assyria," of which, in fact,
it retains the direction. The other arm, which

---

[1] See Loftus, *Chaldæa and Susiania*, pp. 7, 8.

[2] It is this fact which enables the author of Gen. ii. to view the
Lower Tigris as, in some sort, an arm of the Euphrates.

is now considered to be the true Tigris, and which skirted Susiania or " the land of Cush," he called " the Gihon," and viewed as corresponding, in a certain sense, with the Pison, being the extreme eastern river, as that was the extreme western. He commences his enumeration from the west with the stream that skirted Arabia (Havilah) ; he then passes, by the law of parallelism, to the most eastern stream, that which skirted Susiania (Cush, Kissia). Returning westward, he comes to the Tigris (Hiddekel), which he consequently makes the third river, and he concludes with the great river of all (*han-nahar hag-gadōl*), the Euphrates, which is thus first (ver. 10) and last (ver. 14) in his narrative.

II.

ON THE EARLY CITIES OF BABYLONIA.

SACRED and profane history agree in representing Babylonia, or the alluvial plain on the lower courses of the Tigris and Euphrates, as the oldest seat of civilisation in Asia, and the place where a settled government was first set up. At present this alluvial plain, formed by the deposits of the two great rivers during many millennia, is a tract 430 miles long by about 120 miles broad, containing therefore an area of about 50,000 square miles, or a space about equal to that of England without Wales. As, however, the plain is always growing towards the south-east, where it abuts upon the Persian Gulf, through the annual deposits which the rivers bring with them to the sea, whereby the coast-line is continually advancing, it is certain that at the early period at which Babylonian monarchy grew up—4000 or 5000 years ago—the area was considerably smaller. The best authorities are of opinion that at that distant date the Persian Gulf extended inland at least 120 or 130 miles further than at present, so that the length of the alluvium was then not more than about 300 miles, and its area not more than 36,000 square miles. This is a space about equal to that of Portugal, half that of Prussia proper, and considerably larger than that of Bavaria, or Ireland, or Scotland, or the Low Countries.

Naturally this tract was a perfectly level plain, with a slight tilt to the south-west. It was one of enormous productive power; but for the full fertility of the soil to be made available, it was necessary that the water of the two great streams should be artificially spread far and wide over its surface. Until human art supplemented the arrangements of nature, by far the greater portion of the area would have been alternate swamp and desert. Date-groves would, no doubt, have thickly fringed the banks of the main streams, and of any lesser channels into which they may have divided themselves; but the spaces between

the streams, unwatered by springs, and rarely
refreshed by showers, would, excepting in
spring-time, when they must have been in-
undated, have tended to become dry and
parched up, covered only with a coarse grass,
or with low bushes, such as now cover the
level country in many places where it is left
uncultivated.

Still, compared with other regions, the
country would have been one to attract the
regards of primitive man and draw him to
settle in it. Here was a climate which, if
warmer than agreeable in summer, was at any
rate free from any extreme of cold in winter,
and might be inhabited by those whose cloth-
ing was of the scantiest, and whose houses
consisted of wattled huts, formed of willow or
tamarisk boughs and thatched with palm-leaves
or reeds. The date-palm was alone sufficient
to sustain life. Strabo says that it furnished
the Babylonians of his day with " bread, wine,
vinegar, honey, groats, string and ropes of
all kinds, and a mash for fattening cattle." [1]
The fruit is even now the principal food

---

[1] Strab. xvi. 1, § 14.

of the common people in all date-growing countries. The pith was also eaten; a slightly intoxicating liquor was made from the sap; this, on undergoing the acetous fermentation, became vinegar; palm-sugar was obtained from the dried fruit; the bark furnished ropes and string; the timber was employed for building and furniture. According to the native tradition,[1]—which is accepted by Niebuhr[2] and others,—the wheat plant was also here indigenous, and was extraordinarily large and productive. The leaves were as broad as the palm of a man's hand; and the tendency to grow leaves was so great that the Babylonians were accustomed to mow their wheat-fields twice, and then pasture their cattle on them, in order to keep down the blade and induce the plant to run to ear. The return was enormous; on the most moderate computation, it amounted to fifty-fold at the least, and often reached a hundred-fold.[3]

Thus, it was not long after the subsidence of the Noachial Deluge that the Babylonian

---

[1] Berosus, Fr., i. § 1.

[2] *Vorträge über alte Geschichte*, vol. i. p. 21 (ed. of 1847).

[3] Theophrastus, *Hist. Plant.* viii. 7.

alluvium became somewhat densely inhabited, and a city life—already known to mankind before the great catastrophe (Gen. iv. 17: " Chaldean account of the Deluge," col. i. line 11)—was adopted by a considerable portion of the population. The author of Genesis notes this fact in several places. " Nimrod," he tells us, who was the son of Cush and the great-grandson of Noah, " began to be a mighty one in the earth. . . . And the beginning of his kingdom was Babel, and Erech, and Accad, and Calneh, in the land of Shinar " (Gen. x. 8–10). These places are evidently cities, and their foundation is apparently in the fourth generation after the Deluge. A more particular account is given in ch. xi. of the building of one of them, viz., Babel or Babylon :

" The whole earth was of one language and of one speech. And it came to pass, as they journeyed from the east [eastward, R.V.], that they found a plain in the land of Shinar; and they dwelt there. And they said one to another, Go to, let us make brick, and burn them throughly. And they had brick for stone, and slime had they for mortar. And they said, Go to, let us build us a city, and a tower whose top may reach unto heaven : and let us make us a name, lest we be scattered abroad upon the face of the whole earth. And the Lord came down to see the city and the tower, which the children of men builded. And the Lord said, Behold, the people is one [they are one people, R.V.], and they have all one language, and this [is what R.V.] they begin to do ; and now nothing will be restrained [withholden, R.V.] from them which they have imagined [purpose, R.V.] to do. Go to, let us go down, and there confound their language, that they may not understand one another's speech. So the Lord scattered them abroad from thence upon the face of all the earth ; and they left off to build the city. Therefore is [was, R.V.] the name of it called Babel ; because the Lord did there confound the language of all the earth, and from thence did the Lord scatter them abroad upon the face of all the earth " (ch. xi. 1–9).

In the same chapter we find mention of a fifth Babylonian city, called " Ur of the Chaldees " (ch. xi. 28, 31), which, if not of equal antiquity with the other four, is at any rate not much posterior to them, and which possesses a peculiar interest as the birthplace of the " father of the faithful "—the great Hebrew patriarch, Abraham.

Can we locate the several cities here mentioned ? Can we form any notion of their primitive circumstances and condition ? Can we picture to ourselves the life of their inhabitants, and the relations in which the several cities stood, in the early times, one towards another ?

We begin with the most famous—Babylon or Babel. The site of this great city has never ceased to be known from the time of its foundation. It was the chief city of the Lower Mesopotamian region from about B.C. 1600 to B.C. 300, when it had to yield its pre-eminence to Seleucia. From that time it dwindled and declined, until at last it ceased to be inhabited ; but the site always retained the name, and was well known to historians and geographers. Benjamin of Tuleda mentions it in the twelfth century, Abulfeda and Sir John

Maundeville in the fourteenth, Balbi in the sixteenth, Pietro della Valle in the seventeenth. Carsten Niebuhr in 1765 found the spot still called "Ard Babel."[1] Rich, in 1811, Layard in 1850, Oppert in 1852, found the name Babel, or Babil, especially attached to the most striking of the ruins.[2] There is sufficient evidence to satisfy any candid mind, that an uninterrupted tradition among the inhabitants of the region has always pointed out the massive ruins on the Euphrates above Hillah as those of the great city which was so long the mistress of Southern Mesopotamia, and which for a time wielded the sceptre of the world.

The second city of the group mentioned in Gen. x. 10 may be also identified without much difficulty. The native name, which the Hebrews represented by Erech, seems to have been *Uruk.* This the Alexandrian Greeks represented by Orech, and the classical writers, both Greek and Latin, by Orchoë.[3] Orchoë,

---

[1] Niebuhr, *Voyage en Arabie,* vol. ii. p. 234.

[2] Rich, "Journey to Babylon," p. 13; Layard, "Nineveh and Babylon," p. 484; Oppert, *Expédition Scientifique en Mésopotamie,* vol. i. p. 168.

[3] Strabo, xvi. 1, §6; Ptol. v. 20; Plin. *Hist. Nat.* vi. 27.

upon the Arab conquest, was corrupted into Warka ; and this name still attaches to an important group of ruins in the territory of the Montefik Arabs, about five miles east of the Euphrates in lat. 31° 20′. There can be no reasonable doubt that Warka is Erech. It is distant about eighty miles from Babylon in a south-easterly direction, and is about 160 miles from the sea.

Accad, the third city, is not so easy to locate. The Babylonian remains give "Akkad" generally as a country, the more northern portion of Babylonia, that adjoining upon the Assyrian upland. Mr. George Smith, however, the explorer and Assyriologist, found a town in this district, the Babylonian name of which he read as *Agadé*, and this *Agadé* he believed to represent the Biblical " Accad." [1] Agadé was in the immediate vicinity of the modern Sura, which is upon the Euphrates, about eleven or twelve miles above Babylon, on the left bank. It is questioned,[2] however, if the true reading of the name read as Agadé by Mr. Smith is

[1] " History of Babylonia," p. 61.
[2] By Professor Sayce and others.

not rather Agané, in which case the supposed identification would fall to the ground, and the site of " Accad " would be an unsolved problem.

Calneh, the fourth city, which is called Kalanné or Kalané by the LXX. (Gen. x. 10 ; Isa. x. 9), is thought to be the modern " Niffer "[1] situated on the eastern edge of the Affej marshes, between fifty and sixty miles from Babylon towards the south-east. This identification rests mainly on a passage of the Talmud, which says that Calneh was the same place as " Nopher," which is no doubt a variant for " Niffer." The ancient name appears to have been " Nipur ; " and the city may have obtained its variant title of Calneh, or Kal-ana, from its being a main seat of the worship of Ana, one of the chief Babylonian gods. Kal-ana would mean " the fort of the god Ana ; " and just as Asshur, the early capital of Assyria, was known also as Tel-ana,[2] " the hill of Ana," so Nipur may have had a second name of a similar character.

[1] Sir H. Rawlinson in the author's " Herodotus," vol. i. p. 490 (2nd ed.)

[2] Steph. Byz. *ad voc.* Τελάνη.

A tradition, which however can only be traced back to the time of Ephraëm Syrus, A.D. 330–370, identified the " Ur " of Genesis with Orfa, or Orrha, as it appears to have been sometimes called, a town of Upper Mesopotamia, in the near vicinity of Haran or *Harran*. And this identification is still accepted by many. But the tract in which Orfa was situated was never known as Chaldæa, and never even subject to the Chaldees, whether northern or southern, the northern Chaldees dwelling in Eastern Armenia and not being a conquering people, while the southern ones seem never to have held the Upper Mesopotamian tract, which was distant above four hundred miles from their proper country. The Chaldees of Scripture (*Casdim*) are from first to last the people (or a people) of Babylonia, and it is in Babylonia that the earliest Jewish tradition, that recorded by Eupolemus,[1] about B.C. 150, places Ur, or " Uria," as he calls it, the home of Abraham. Modern research has found in this region an ancient Babylonian city which bore the identical name of Ur, or

[1] Ap. Euseb. *Præp. Ev.* ix. 17.

rather 'Ur, the Babylonian literation exactly corresponding to the Hebrew, which is אור. The ruins of this place bear at present the name of Mugheir, or " the bitumened," from the great quantity of bitumen found in them. They are situated on the right bank of the Euphrates, at the distance of about six miles from the stream, nearly opposite the point where the Euphrates receives the Shat-el-Hie from the Tigris. They are distant from Warka (Erech) forty miles, from Niffer (Calneh) about ninety miles, from Babylon about 150 miles.

A great uniformity of character attaches to all these sites. The early inhabitants seem to have regarded two things as necessary conditions to render a place suitable for their abode. In the first place, it must be within a reasonable distance of the Euphrates, or of some branch stream ; in the second, it must be slightly elevated above the general level of the plain, so as to escape the inundation which almost every spring covers the greater part of the low country. Although the alluvium is, in a general way, level, yet it presents certain natural inequalities, the result of the water action of many centuries, of the currents, eddies, changes in the beds of streams, &c., which have caused slight elevations in certain places, and considerable depressions in others. These depressions are under water for a third part of the year,[1] and are therefore unsuited for habitations. They are throughout the year marshy and unhealthy, though valuable on account of their products. These consist of huge reeds, and also of game of all kinds— lions, pelicans, francolins, king-fishers, and various species of water-fowl.[2] The reeds furnish materials for huts and boats, and were doubtless utilised by the primitive people before they were sufficiently advanced in civilisation to mould bricks and harden them in kilns or furnaces. The present life of the Affej Arabs gives probably a fair idea of the condition and habits of the earliest dwellers in Babylonia.

"The Affej towns consist entirely of reed huts, the reeds being tied in large bundles, and

---

[1] Loftus, "Chaldæa and Susiana," p. 92.
[2] Layard, "Nin. and Bab." pp. 350-353.

neatly arched overhead. This primitive construction is covered externally with thick matting, impervious to rain. The riches of the Affej are indicated by rows of huge reed cylindrical baskets, containing the grain upon which they subsist. Rice is produced in great abundance along the edges of the marsh ; but the whole of the fields were at the season of our visit . . . entirely under water. Communication is kept up, as on the marshes of the Hindieh, by means of long, sharp, pointed terrádas, constructed of teak, and measuring 12 or 14 feet long by a yard in width."[1] Others, as Sir Austin Layard tells us, " consist simply of a very narrow framework of rushes covered with bitumen, resembling probably the vessels of bulrushes mentioned by Isaiah (ch. xviii. 2). They skim over the surface of the water with great rapidity."[2] In their Chaldæan wars the Assyrians came upon tribes in exactly this condition, and faithfully delineated the scenes upon their bas-reliefs.[3]

[1] Loftus, "Chaldæa and Susiana," p. 92.
[2] Layard, " Nineveh and Babylon," p. 552.
[3] Layard, "Monuments of Nineveh," 2nd series, Pls. 25, 27, and 28.

C

But the ingenuity of the primitive Babylonians soon carried them beyond such rude
and simple constructions. Possessing no
metals, which Babylonia did not produce,
they contrived to make themselves axes,
hammers, knives, and planes of stone and
flint, wherewith they succeeded in cutting
down palm-trees, and shaping them into
beams, door-posts, planks, and even boats.
Wooden houses took the place of the earlier
reed hovels, the roof and supports being probably of timber, and the outer walls perhaps of
plaster or clay.   Houses of this character still
exist in the Mesopotamian region, especially
among the Yezidi of the Sinjar. "The best
house in the village," says Sir A. Layard, "had
been made ready for us, and was scrupulously
neat and clean, as the houses of the Yezidis
usually are.   It was curiously built, being
divided into three principal rooms opening
one into another.   They were separated by a
wall about six feet high, on which were placed
wooden pillars supporting the ceiling. The
roof rested on trunks of trees, raised on rude
stone pedestals at regular intervals in the

centre chamber, which was open on one side to the air, like a Persian Iwan. The sides of the room were honeycombed with small recesses, like pigeon-holes, tastefully arranged. The whole was plastered with the whitest plaster, fancy designs in bright red being introduced here and there, giving the interior of the house a very original appearance."[1] Similar designs have been found on some walls of very early Babylonian buildings; sometimes they consist of mere bands about three inches wide, alternately red, black, and white, but occasionally they represent figures, animal and human.[2]

Even, however, habitations of this superior kind did not long content the Babylonians. Greater permanency became an object of desire; a more secure protection against heat and rain was felt to be needed. In most countries these wants lead early to the erection of edifices of stone, the most lasting material that is widely diffused over the earth's surface. But in Babylonia, speaking gene-

---

[1] "Nineveh and Babylon," p. 252.
[2] "Journal of R. Asiatic Society," vol. xv. pp. 408 and 410.

rally, there was no stone. Except on the
verge of the Arabian desert, which is strewn
with fragments of black basalt, and on the
skirts of the Kebir Kuh and Pushti Kuh, if
the tract east of the Tigris may be reckoned to
Babylonia, stone was absolutely wanting, the
soil consisting everywhere of a deep alluvial
deposit, chiefly clay and loam, with occasional
sand and gravel. The Babylonians were
therefore precluded from following the architectural example of most other nations. In
this difficulty they found a material, in some
respects superior to stone, more tractable,
more easy of conveyance, and almost more
lasting, which was everywhere ready to their
hand, and by means of which they were able
to erect solid, durable, and magnificent constructions. This material was brick. The
clay with which the alluvium abounds is of
a most tenacious character, and even when
merely exposed to the heat of the sun becomes
so firm and hard as to be a very tolerable
building material ; when kiln-baked, it is a
very compact substance indeed, and may be

pronounced superior to most kinds of stone in respect of enduringness.

The earliest of the existing Babylonian ruins are of sun-dried brick ; but burnt brick was also used from a very remote period, ordinarily as a facing to the inferior material, which formed the mass of each edifice. Walls were commonly of great thickness, probably to keep out the heat ; and buildings of any pretension were usually emplaced upon mounds, the intention being (probably) in part to secure them against the danger of inundation, in part to elevate them into an atmosphere above that most frequented by the gnats and mosquitoes, which are among the chief plagues of hot marshy regions. Temples, which were the habitations of the powerful priest-class, especially affected a superior altitude. They occupied commonly the summit of a sort of truncated pyramid, built in stages, which occasionally were as many as seven. Flights of steps led up from one stage to another, the last flight conducting the visitor to the shrine itself, which was small but rich in its ornamentation. The houses in Babylon itself were, we are told,[1] of several stories in height, the object being doubtless the same, to reach a rarer atmosphere, above the ordinary flight of the insects.

There must have been a general resemblance among most of the Babylonian cities. Embosomed in groves of palms, with orchards and gardens both without and within the walls, they were centres from which the cultivation of cereals was carried on, so far as the water from the streams on which they were situated could be carried. Nature provided an abundance of the life-giving fluid. It was probably at an early date that the art of man was called in to assist in its greater diffusion, and canals began to be cut in the soft soil, for the purpose of irrigating the tracts that lay at some distance from the river. A monarch who cannot be placed much later than B.C. 1600, has left an inscription commemorating his excavation of a great canal, which he calls "a stream of abundant waters, the joy of men."[2] He was not, however, the first to engage in a work of this kind—the task which

[1] Herod. i. 180.   [2] See "Records of the Past," vol. i. p. 7.

he set himself was, he tells us, to restore rather than to create. " The canal of Khammurabi," he says, " for the people of Sumir and Accad I excavated. Its banks, all of them I restored to newness ; new supporting walls I heaped up ; perennial waters for the people of Sumir and Accad I provided." [1] At a later time the whole country became covered with a network of artificial channels, by means of which the precious fluid was conveyed to all parts of the territory.

One city, however, was somewhat peculiarly situated. The town called 'Ur, which we identify with the scriptural " Ur of the Chaldees," was situated so low down the stream of the Euphrates that it was practically the port Babylonia. It was at first either actually on the shore of the Gulf, or at any rate but a very short distance removed from it. Hence the inscriptions constantly speak of " the ships of Ur," and represent the inhabitants as engaged largely in commerce. A brisk trade was doubtless carried on from exceedingly remote times between the various dwellers upon the

[1] See " Records of the Past," vol. i. p. 7.

Gulf—Babylonians, Arabs, Elamites—and it is not unlikely that there was some early communication between the Mesopotamian emporium, 'Ur, and the distant countries of India, Ethiopia, and Egypt.

In the most ancient times to which the Babylonian monuments carry us back, the entire country did not form a single organised monarchy. The great cities, 'Ur, Erech, Nipur, Larsa, Babel, &c., were for the most part capitals of distant and separate states, each ruled by its own native kings. Wars between the different states were frequent, and sometimes they had to submit themselves, one and all, to the dominion of a foreign conqueror. It was not till about the seventeenth century before our era that consolidation took place, and the six or seven states which had for many centuries divided Babylonia among them became united into a single monarchy, under a line of kings who fixed their capital at Babylon.[1]

---

[1] G. Smith, "History of Babylonia," p. 81.

III.

ON THE CHIEF CITIES OF ANCIENT ASSYRIA.

THE writer of Genesis passes, in ver. 11 of chap. x., from the chief cities of Babylonia to those of Assyria, which he declares to be three or four, according as we translate the passage. If we follow the interpretation of the Septuagint, the cities will be four, " Nineveh, Rehoboth, Calah, and Resen" (Dasé, LXX.) ; if we accept that of the Vulgate, they will be reduced to three, " Nineveh, Calah, Resen." We prefer the latter interpretation, since it would be very strange if out of a list of four cities one alone should have the word " city " attached to it, and since the statement in ver. 12, that " Resen lay between Nineveh and Calah," seems to imply that the writer has in his mind, and is bent on locating, three cities only.   We take " Rehoboth 'ir " to mean " the streets of the city," *i.e.* of Nineveh, with the Vulgate and with the margin of the Authorised Version.

Nineveh, the capital of Assyria during its most flourishing period, was situated upon the Tigris, according to the concurrent testimony of Herodotus,[1] Ctesias,[2] Strabo,[3] and Ptolemy.[4] Though utterly ruined and devoid of inhabitants from the close of the seventh century B.C. to about A.D. 40, tradition seems to have handed down its site, and when it became a fortified post under the Parthians, the old name was applied to the new fortress.[5] Claudius, whose *protegé*, Meherdates, took it in A.D. 49, gave it the dignity of a Roman colony, and this rank was also allowed it by Trajan (A.D. 116) and Maximin (A.D. 235).[6] In B.C. 627, Heraclius occupied it in his war with Chosroës.[7] The early Arab geographers mention it as *Ninawi*, and several of the early

---

[1] Herod. i. 193,

[2] Ctesias was probably the source of the Assyrian history of Nic. Damasc., who places Nineveh upon the Tigris, Fr. 9.

[3] Strabo, xvi. 1, § 1.   [4] Ptol. *Geograph.* vi. 1.

[5] Tacit. *Annales*, xii. 13.

[6] As appears by their coins (Layard, "Nineveh and Babylon," p. 591).

[7] Theophanes, "Chronograph," p. 367 A.

European travellers, as Benjamin of Tudela,
Purchas, and Carsten Niebuhr, found the name
still in use. Their notices, combined with
those of the ancient geographers, produced—
long ere recent explorations commenced—a
general *consensus* as to the situation of the
city, which was identified with the ruins
opposite Mosul by Assemani, Brotier, and
many others.

The excavations of recent travellers, par-
ticularly those of Sir A. Layard and Mr. Loftus,
have completely confirmed the traditional
identification. The town, of which the chief
remains are those at Nebbi-Yunus and Koyunjik, opposite Mosul, is found to have borne
the name of "Ninua," and to have been the
main capital of the later Assyrian kings, especially of Sennacherib and Asshur-bani-pal.
The present ruins, which are all that can be
safely regarded as belonging to the ancient
city, consist of " an enclosure formed by a
continuous line of mounds, resembling a vast
embankment of earth, but marking the remains
of a wall, the western face of which is inter-
rupted by the two great mounds of Koyunjik

and Nebbi-Yunus. To the east of this enclosure are the remains of an extensive line of defences, consisting of moats and ramparts. The inner wall forms an irregular quadrangle with very unequal sides, the northern being 2333 yards, the eastern (where the wall is almost the segment of a circle) 5300 yards, the western, or the river face, 4533 yards, and the southern but little more than 1000; altogether 13,200 yards, or seven English miles and four furlongs. The present height of this earthen wall is between forty and fifty feet."[1] The area within the wall is reckoned at 1800 English acres.

It is the opinion of some that the site here described as that of Nineveh itself is that rather of "the royal city" or quarter, and that the town occupied a far more extended area. Sir Austin Layard suggests that an irregular quadrangle, marked at its four corners by the ruins at Shereef Khan, Khorsabad, Nimrud, and Keremles, may better represent the true size of the ancient town,[2] while M. Jules

---

[1] Layard in Dr. W. Smith's "Dict. of the Bible," vol. ii. p. 548.
[2] Layard, "Nineveh and its Remains," vol. ii. p. 247.

Oppert, though not going so far in some respects, gives it an indefinite extension towards the west, on the right bank of the Tigris, and an area about half that suggested by Sir A. Layard on the left bank.[1] The motive of these suggestions is apparently to save the credit of Diodorus Siculus, or of his authority Ctesias, who gave the city a circumference of 480 stades, or 55 miles, whereas the ruins opposite Mosul have one of less than 8 miles. But the veracity of Ctesias has long since been impeached by the best critics, and in relating the size of Nineveh, which had been destroyed and depopulated more than two centuries before his time, he could but be following a vague and uncertain rumour.

The tract in which Nineveh was situated was one of much beauty and fertility. The plain to the east of the Tigris, in the latitude of Mosul (36° 20′), is diversified with many ranges of hills, watered by many streams, wooded in places, and within sight of the Kurdish mountains. The soil is richly productive, and is cultivated at the present day

---

[1] *Expédition scientifique en Mésopotamie*, vol. i. pp. 289, 290.

in corn, cotton, tobacco, and rice.[1]   Oleanders
and myrtles clothe the banks of the clear
and sparkling streams.   Spreading walnuts
and other trees of large size furnish a grateful
shade to the traveller.   The spring rains are
sufficient to produce everywhere abundant
harvests ; and where there is facility for irrigation, gardens bear their fruits during the
greater portion of the year.   Gazelles, wolves,
hyænas, and wild boars frequent many portions of the region,[2] and attract the regards of
the sportsman.

Nineveh was placed at the confluence of the
Khauser or Khosr with the Tigris, and thus
enjoyed the advantage of being watered by
two streams.   The Tigris washed its western
face, and glassed in its waters the glories of
its principal palaces.   The Khosr, anciently
called the " Tibilti," or "stream of fertility,"
after flowing for a time nearly parallel to its
eastern rampart, turned suddenly to the west,
and entered the town itself, which it divided
into two portions.   Ordinarily a sluggish

---

[1] Layard, " Nineveh and Babylon," pp. 77, 367.
[2] *Ibid.* pp. 173, 175.

stream, and flowing in a deep bed, it was liable after heavy rains to become a brawling torrent, overflowing its banks, and carrying all before it. Sennacherib tells us that in his time "the River Tibilti had ruined the brick-work of the royal palace when it ravaged the quays of the ancient city. For a long time the river had undermined the front of the palace. In the high water of its floods it had made great rents in the foundations, and had washed away the *timin*" (?). Under these circumstances Sennacherib pulled down what remained of the ancient palace, dug a new channel for the Khosr, which he guarded on either side by a strong wall, regulated the flow of the stream by artificial means, prob-ably dams and sluices, and then proceeded to rebuild the palace on a higher platform and with enlarged dimensions. Around it he tells us that he planted "the finest of trees, equal to those of the land of Khamana (Mount Amanus), which all who are knowing in trees prefer to any that grow in Chaldæa."[1]

The second city of Assyria, according to the

[1] "Records of the Past," vol. i. pp. 30, 31.

writer of Genesis, was Calah, or rather Calakh. Though unnoticed as a city by the Greek and Roman geographers, Calah must undoubtedly have given name to the province called Calachêné, or Calaciné,[1] which lay north of Adiabêné, or the country between the two Zab rivers. The city, however, destroyed at the same time with Nineveh, passed into complete oblivion soon afterwards, and apart from the decipherment of the cuneiform inscriptions, its site could not possibly have been recovered. But one of the best ascertained results of the researches made among the Mesopotamian mounds is the attachment of the name of Calah to the great mounds at Nimrud,[2] which are only second to those opposite Mosul for size and importance. The name of the city reads on all its inscriptions as "Kalkhu;" and the inscriptions show that in the middle Assyrian period, from about B.C. 883 to B.C. 719, it was the principal capital, and the ordi-

---

[1] Calachêné by Strabo (xvi. 1. § 1), Calaciné by Ptolemy ("Geograph." vi. 1).

[2] Oppert says, "L'identification de Calah avec les ruines de Nimrud est une chose acquise à la science, et n'est plus contestée" (*Expédition scientifique en Mésopotamie*, vol. i. p. 309).

nary residence of the monarchs. The position of Calah and its site are thus described by M. Jules Oppert :—

" The ruins of Nimrud are distant from those of Nineveh between twenty-nine and thirty kilometres towards the south, and are situated, like the Nineveh ruins, on the left bank of the Tigris. This river has, from a remote period, undergone important changes in its course. At the present time it flows at the distance of two kilometres from Nimrud, but anciently it washed the wall of the town ; and the locality still shows signs of the ancient bed. Nimrud, the ancient Calah, retains in their entirety its walls and circumvallations. Formerly washed by the Tigris along the entire length of its western face, which measures 1450 metres, and extending almost as far along the side which looks to the south-west, the town presents an irregular figure of six sides, with receding angles. The northern portion is bounded by a wall nearly 2000 metres in length, which runs from east to west ; another wall runs from north to south, nearly in a straight line, but with a slight deflection to the east, for a distance of 1300 metres, meeting then a wall parallel to the first, which runs from east to west for 750 metres. If prolonged sufficiently, this wall would meet the western face, and would thus form a pretty regular oblong; but, instead, the wall turns at an obtuse angle, and runs towards the south-south-west, where anciently it met the Tigris, which here flowed to the south-east. A branch wall, projecting itself from this, ran to the E.S.E. in the direction of four tumuli now called *Tolul Yazar*. This piece of ground formed an irregular square bordered on one side by an affluent of the Tigris, and seems to have been a sort of suburb. The entire town occupied altogether a space of exactly 300 hectares" (742 acres).[1]

The site of Resen is still an unsolved problem. It has been identified by some with Ras-el-Ain, on the Khabour in Western Mesopotamia;[2] but nothing is more clear than that the Resen of Gen. x. 11, 12 was on the eastern side of the Tigris, in the vicinity

---

[1] Oppert, *Expédition Scientifique*, vol. i. p. 309.
[2] Winer, *Realwörterbuch, ad voc.* RESEN.

of Nineveh and Calah. The writer says that it lay "between" those towns, which, if taken strictly, must place it in the same latitude, Calah being due south of Nineveh; if taken with less strictness, must still place it in the same region, not very far out of the direct route. On the former supposition, Selamiyeh is the most probable site; on the latter, Keremles or Balawat. Selamiyeh, however, being within three miles of Nimrud, can scarcely have been "a great city" while Nimrud was in its full glory, and must therefore be set aside, in which case the choice would seem to lie between Balawat and Kerem les. The ruins at these places are not very extensive, and modern research has not recovered the ancient name of either; but Balawat seems to have been a place of some consequence,[1] and is therefore perhaps to be preferred. Another possibility is that Resen early went to decay, and that at present there are no remains of it. It is to be borne in

[1] See the papers of Mr. Hormuzd Rassam and Mr. Pinches in the "Transactions of the Society of Bibl. Archæology," vol. vii. pp. 37-118.

mind that the name does not occur in the
native legends.

The character of the Assyrian towns is
remarkable. Though built in a region where
stone is plentiful, and crops out frequently
upon the surface, stone is used very sparingly
in them as a material. The outer wall of a
town was indeed sometimes constructed of
solid stone masonry up to a certain height,[1]
and slabs of stone were employed both for
pavements and for the lining of chambers,
gateways, and the like ; but the chief material
whereof buildings of all kinds were constructed
was, as in Babylonia, brick—either sun-dried
or kiln-baked. This unnatural proceeding can
only be explained as the result of habit. If
the builders were emigrants from a region
that possessed no stone, and had been long
accustomed to make all their edifices of brick,
they might find it simpler and easier to pro-
ceed in their habitual manner than to adopt
new methods and seek to deal with an un-
familiar and intractable material. Now this

---

[1] Layard, "Nineveh and Babylon," p. 123; Rawlinson, "Ancient
Monarchies," vol. i. p. 349.

exactly accords with what we are told in Genesis—"Out of that land" (*i.e.*, Babylonia, which had no stone) " went forth Asshur, and builded Nineveh, and the streets of the city, and Calah, and Resen between Nineveh and Calah : the same is a great city." Asshur, *i.e.*, the Assyrian nation, brought with it into Assyria the arts which it had learnt in Babylonia, and only modified them slightly in consequence of its new environment.

Among the modifications made, the principal was the substitution of a new wall ornamentation for the old one which had prevailed in the more southern country. The Babylonians, anxious to beautify the interiors of their grander edifices, had invented the art of enamelling bricks, and were wont to cover their temple and palace walls with coloured representations of their kings and queens engaged in war or in the chase.[1] The Assyrians, finding that their hill ranges furnished a delicate material, easily worked, in the shape of a sort of grey alabaster of a fine quality, quarried this material extensively, and having

[1] Diod. Sic. ii. 8. § 6 ; Ezek. xxiii. 14–16.

first carved on it in low relief scenes similar to those wherewith their residence in Babylonia had made them familiar, proceeded to colour them delicately and with much taste. The pigments used were applied to certain parts of the figures only, as to the hair, the eyes, and the beards of men, to the trappings and hoofs of horses, to the royal tiara and parasol, to the fringes of dresses, the shafts of spears and arrows, the stems and branches of trees, to bows, belts, fillets, quivers, maces, reins, sandals, flowers held in the hand, and the like, the object being to give greater distinctness to the scenes represented, by disentangling human from animal figures, dress from flesh, or human figures from one another. The effect was probably exceedingly good, and is unfortunately lost, now that the slabs have in almost every instance been entirely denuded of the colouring materials by the long course of time and the wear and tear to which they have been subjected.

Besides the material whereof they are mainly constructed, the Assyrian cities furnish some other evidence of their builders' Babylonian proclivities. The builders selected for the sites of their cities flat places on or near the courses of rivers, avoiding the natural elevations, which were plentiful throughout the greater portion of the country; and then, having made this choice, they proceeded, like the Babylonians, to construct artificial elevations, on which to emplace their more dignified and important buildings. The plague of insects is not great in the upper Mesopotamian regions; the rivers do not overflow their banks as a general rule; and thus the reasons which impelled the Babylonians to build their temples and palaces on lofty mounds were wanting. But the force of habit, perhaps aided by sentiment, prevailed. According to the ideas prevalent at the time, the proper site for a great city was a plain (Gen. xi. 2–4); and it was proper that the principal buildings should look down on the rest of the city from elevations. Artificial mounds were accordingly constructed, either of unbaked brick or of earth and rubbish, with a revetement of stone or burnt brick; and these elevations are as universal on Assyrian sites as on Babylonian ones.

Where a palace or temple platform lay on the outer circuit of an Assyrian town, no other defence was necessary, for the sides of the platforms were perpendicular, and formed of solid blocks of hewn stone, or else of a very hard and smooth-baked brick. Where circumstances allowed, however, the further defence of a water barrier was interposed between the town and any possible assailant, and a similar defence was carried along the foot of the walls, a deep ditch being dug, which was kept filled with water. In one instance such a ditch has been quarried for upwards of two miles through a great mass of compact conglomerate rock ;[1] and this forms an outer defence additional to the usual wall and moat. But in general a single moat and a single wall were thought sufficient. The wall was strengthened at intervals by towers, which projected slightly, and enabled the defenders to take their assailants in flank ; it had also necessarily to be pierced at intervals by gateways, to allow of ingress and egress. Such gateways were constructed with great

---

[1] "Journal of the Royal Asiatic Society," vol. xv. p. 320.

care, and were guarded by strong garrisons, and closed with gates of solid wood coated with bronze.[1]

The rivers of Assyria run in deep beds, and the country between them is elevated considerably above their level. Canalisation on any large scale is thus difficult, if not impossible ; and anciently there was a very marked difference between the low flat Babylonia, with its complicated network of channels for irrigation, and the undulating Assyrian upland, with its numerous ranges of limestone and conglomerate hills, which depended mainly on the spring rains for its fertility, and admitted of irrigation in comparatively few places. Assyria grew scarcely any dates. Its principal trees were the sycamore, the Oriental plane, the walnut, and the silver poplar. It had also an abundance of palms of the unproductive kind. The land was suitable for the growth of corn, and still more for gardens and orchards. It bore the vine, the olive, the fig, the pomegranate, the plum, the

---

[1] Layard, "Nineveh and Babylon," p. 122; "Transactions of Society of Bibl. Archæology," vol. vii. p. 85.

pear, the apple, the palma Christi,[1] and the
pistachio nut. Vines were either grown as
standards, or else trained upon trees, as we see
them in the sculptures of Asshur-bani-pal.[2]
Grapes and pomegranates were favourite
fruits, and graced the banquets of the kings.

The Assyrian towns do not seem to have
contained many houses of much pretension.
Within the enceintes of Nineveh, Calah, and
Dur-Sargina (Khorsabad)—the three principal
cities of the later kingdom—there are scarcely
any remains except those of palaces and temples. Neither stone nor burned brick can
have been much used in the habitations of the
common people, which were probably of sun-
dried brick or of wood, and easily perished
without leaving a trace behind them. Many
of the labouring class in the country districts
may even have dwelt in " booths," such as
that which Jonah constructed for himself,
when waiting to see what would befall the
city which he had been commissioned to de-
nounce.[3]

---

[1] The " gourd " of Jonah iii. 6–10.
[2] "Ancient Monarchies," vol. i. p. 439.   [3] Jonah iii. 5.

Assyria anciently abounded with lions, which found ample covert in the jungle that fringed the banks of the Tigris; with wild boars, which haunted various reedy districts, and sometimes wrought havoc in the gardens; with gazelles, which roamed in herds over the plains intervening between the Tigris and the Zagros mountains; with hares, which were common everywhere, with partridges of several kinds, and with various sorts of wild fowl. Deer and bears were found on the skirts of Zagros; the ibex or wild goat was tolerably plentiful in places; and on the Mesopotamian plain south of the Sinjar range it was possible to meet with wild asses and with ostriches.[1] Thus the country was one very apt to develop the instincts of the sportsman; and from a very early time the example of Nimrod seems to have been followed by many of its inhabitants. Several of the kings were " mighty hunters," and passed the intervals between their campaigns mainly in the chase of the lion, the wild ass, and the

---

[1] Xen. *Anab.* i. 5, § 2, 3.

ibex or wild goat. The courtiers and other nobles followed naturally the example thus set them; and a considerable section of the population was drawn into this class of pursuits.

IV.

ELAM, ITS CHIEF CITY, AND ITS CHIEF RIVER.

THE history of Abraham introduces to the reader of Scripture a new country, apparently of great importance, which bears the name of Elam. Elam does not appear as a country in the earlier chapters of Genesis, where Babylonia, Assyria, and Egypt hold the chief place (Gen. ii. 14, x. 8–12, xi. 2–9, xii. 10–20). But soon after Abraham had settled himself in Hebron (ib. chap. xiii. 18), the power and importance of Elam is shown very remarkably. An Elamite monarch, named "Chedorlaomer," or "Chodol-logomer" (LXX.), led an expedition into Palestine from some region of the far East, adjoining (it would seem) on Babylonia,[1] and made a conquest of the Jordan

---

[1] One of Chedorlaomer's confederate kings is Amraphel king of Shinar, *i.e.*, Babylonia), another is Arioch king of Ellasar (*i.e.*, Larsa, a Babylonian city).

valley, which he held for twelve years (Gen. xiv. 1–4). The kings of Sodom, Gomorrah, Admah, Zeboiim, and Zoar "served Chedorlaomer," were his subjects and tributaries, for that space of time. Then they turned and "rebelled" against him (ib. ver. 4), and Chedorlaomer made a second expedition into the Palestinian region, defeated the kings, and re-established his authority over them. Abraham, however, hearing that he had taken his nephew, Lot, prisoner, " armed his trained servants" (ib. ver. 14), and hanging upon Chedorlaomer's rear, succeeded in recovering his nephew, and those belonging to him, who would otherwise have been carried off to the distant Elam (ver. 16).

Elsewhere in Scripture Elam appears as the " province," or district, in which "Shushan" (Susa) was situated (Dan. viii. 2), as watered by the river Ulai (ib.), as subject to Assyria in the time of Esar-haddon (Ezra iv. 2, 9), and as participating in the final destruction of Babylon (Isa. xxi. 2). These notices sufficiently identify it with the Elymais of the Greeks and Romans, and the Elam, or Elam-ti, of the Assyrians.[1] The cuneiform inscriptions show, that from the earliest historical period, and thenceforth to the destruction of Assyria, there was always a third power in the Mesopotamian lowland, situated on the left bank of the Lower Tigris, between that stream and the mountains, which long contended for the mastery, on almost equal terms, with Babylonia and Assyria. This country, which the Greeks and Romans called generally Susiana from its capital, and which is now known as Khuzistan, extended from the Persian Gulf and the river Tigris, a distance of 100 or 120 miles, to the foot of the Bakhtiyari mountains, and stretched along the range as much as 300 miles. It is a region of a very varied character. Along the Persian Gulf and the course of the Tigris is a low flat plain of " saliferous alluvium," [2] extending a distance of some 70 miles, very marshy in places, and, excepting along the courses of the rivers, ill suited for cultivation. Camel's thorn and tamarisk are the chief vegetable productions,

---

[1] See G. Smith's "History of Asshur-bani-pal," pp. 100–253.
[2] Loftus, " Chaldæa and Susiana," p. 290.

the latter growing luxuriantly along the banks of the streams, where also occasionally is to be seen "a deep grove of palm-trees."[1] The heat is great in the whole of this district, which, where it is not a marsh, is for the most part an arid desert. It can at no time have sustained more than a scanty population. On quitting the lower plains the traveller enters a tract of undulating ground, belonging to the tertiary formation, in which beds of sandstone and gravel alternate, and the vegetation undergoes a sensible improvement. After the winter rains, which last from December to March, the entire surface of the ground puts on a livery of green, diversified with numerous brilliant flowers, and a rich pasturage is everywhere afforded to the flocks and herds of the inhabitants. The whole country is "plentifully studded with green konar trees,"[2] with their bright red berries ; a species of oak is found in places, which grows to the height of 40 or 50 feet; oleanders, with their delicate pink blossoms fringe the courses of the streams,

[1] Loftus, "Chaldæa and Susiana," p. 288.
[2] Ibid., p. 293.

while occasionally in a dried-up river-bed is seen a perfect forest of tamarisk, poplar, and acacia, or a dense mass of date-trees, konars, and jungle enshrouds a building. Rare shrubs and fruit-bearing plants, strange to European eyes, diversify the scene; in places the air is heavy with the scent of orange and lemon trees, and the rich soil yields everywhere to the cultivator abundant crops of corn, rice, grapes, melons, cucumbers, and indigo. The heat, though considerable, ceases to be oppressive. In the distance can be seen the snow-clad range of Bakhtiyari mountains, rising to an elevation of from 8000 to 10,000 feet above the level of the sea, in a continuous undulating line void of peaks or of any prominent features, while the breeze which blows from them is almost always cool and refreshing. The temperature, as measured by the thermometer, is high, especially during the middle of the day, when the natives retire to their *serdaubs*, or underground apartments; but, on the whole, the climate is spoken of as "delightful," [1] at any rate compared with that of the lower region.

[1] Loftus, p. 307.

E

The Bakhtiyari mountain region, which impends over the Elamitic plain, which modifies its climate to such an important extent, and is so prominent a geographical feature to all who traverse it, was probably in ancient times to a certain distance Elamitic territory. The Elamites are by Strabo regarded as mountaineers,[1] and '*al*, the root of Elam, means "high," "elevated." This great range, which is from 50 to 100 miles broad, consists of a number of ridges, "rising in huge, elongated saddles of compact altered limestone, parallel to each other."[2]   Between the ridges flow streams in courses from north-east to south-west, or *vice versâ*, uniting their waters ultimately into large rivers, which burst their way through the several limestone barriers, and passing through a number of "tangs," or gorges, descend upon the plain in a direction which is generally somewhat west of south.[3] "Scarped rocks rise almost perpendicularly on either side of the mountain streams, which descend rapidly with frequent cascades and falls."[4]   To reach the Iranian upland on the further side of the

[1] *Geograph.*, xi. 13, § 6 ; xvi. 1, § 17.   [2] Loftus, p. 308.
[3] Loftus, p. 309.   [4] "Ancient Monarchies," vol. iv. p. 9.

barrier, it is necessary to climb the successive ridges by roads scarcely better than goat-tracks, which regular gradation of ascents was expressed by the Greek historians and geographers under the term κλίμακες, or " ladders." The roads are carried in zig-zags along the slight irregularities of the precipitous rocks, often crossing the streams from side to side by bridges of a single arch, which are thrown over profound chasms where the waters chafe and rage many hundreds of feet below. " Superimposed on the hard limestone rocks are beds of a softer nature—marls rivalling the coloured sands of our own Isle of Wight in their brilliant and variegated aspect, vast piles of amorphous gypsum dazzling the eye with its excessive whiteness, and successive layers of red sands alternating with gravel." [1]   Mountain, valley, and upland plain succeed each other throughout the region. On the highest ridges snow remains throughout the year, and elsewhere it is often found in crevices.   The upper flanks of the mountains are bare, but the lower are clothed with

---

[1] Loftus, p. 308.

wood, or cultivated in cereals, while the valleys teem with orchards and gardens, and the upland plains furnish excellent pasture.[1] The character of the region deteriorates, however, towards the south-east, where it adjoins upon the ancient Persia, the mountains becoming barer and more arid, and the valleys narrower and less fertile.

A chief feature of the Elamitic plain are the rivers by which it is traversed. Five main streams debouch from the mountains into the Elamitic lowland—the Dwarij, the Kerkhah, the river of Dizful, the Kuran, and the Jerahi. The Dwarij is the most western, and the smallest of the five; it rises in the Pushti-Kuh, about lat. 32° 40′, and flows into the Tigris through the Beni Lam marshes. Next in succession is the Kerkhah, a copious stream, never less than 80 yards wide from the point where it enters upon the plain after its junction with the Abi-Zal.[2] Thirdly comes the Diz, or river of Dizful, another copious stream, which approaches the Kerkhah within

---

[1] See "Geographical Journal," vol. ix. pp. 93-97 ; "Ancient Monarchies," vol. iii. pp. 245, 246.

[2] "Ancient Monarchies," vol. iii. p. 270.

a distance of ten miles in the vicinity of Susa. Further east, and flowing from the east, is the Kuran or river of Shuster, which debouches on the plain near that place, and then dividing into two channels flows southward, and joins the Dizful river near Bendikir.[1] The Kuran is a very large stream, and, when increased by the waters of the Diz, becomes the largest river of these parts, "exceeding in size the Tigris and Euphrates."[2] It runs to the south-west from Bendikir, and joins the Shat-el-Arab at Mohammerah. Last of all comes the Jerahi, which has a general western direction as far as Dorak, and carries a considerable body of water, but being there drained by a number of canals, becomes a small stream, and flows nearly due south into the Persian Gulf at Gadi. Between the Kerkhah and the river of Dizful is a sixth stream, known as the Shapur or Shaour, which runs to the south-east, and enters the Dizful river before its junction with the Kuran at Bendikir.

The Elamitic rivers run chiefly in deep channels. They are, for the most part, copious

---

[1] Loftus, p. 292.　　　[2] " Geograph. Journal," vol. xvi. p. 52.

and rapid streams, able to cut deep even into conglomerate rock, and are often skirted by cliffs of considerable elevation.[1] The alluvium, through which they chiefly run, offers them still less resistance than the tertiary formations, and their banks in the lower plain are thus almost always high, though sometimes shelving. Where canals are drawn from them, it is generally necessary to dam up the water by a *bund* or embankment.

The situation chosen for the capital city of Elam was the upper portion of the undulating plain at the foot of the mountains, in the near vicinity of two of the principal rivers, the Kerkhah and the river of Dizful. The Shapur also flowed in the same neighbourhood, while a branch of the Kerkhah, known as the Ulai or Eulæus, thrown off at Pai Pul, 20 miles above the city, seems likewise to have traversed the plain in the near vicinity.[2] Thus the city and its neighbourhood was most copiously supplied with the life-giving fluid, and the fertility of the soil being great, abundant provisions could be raised without

---

[1] Loftus, pp. 311, 314, &c.   [2] Ibid., pp. 424–431.

difficulty to support a large population. The
site, however, tended to be marshy ; and the
earliest inhabitants of Elam must, like those
of Babylonia, have felt the necessity of em-
placing their habitations upon mounds in
order to secure them against inundations.
The ruins of Susa are found to consist of
"four spacious artificial platforms, distinctly
separate from each other." The most elevated
of these is towards the west, and is washed
by the Shapur, the green waters of which
meander through a dense mass of vegetation.
It attains a height of 119 feet above the river,
and is believed to have been the ancient
acropolis, or citadel. To the north of this is
a square mass, about 1000 feet each way,
which was certainly the site of the royal
palace in Persian times. South-east of these
two mounds, and much exceeding in size both
of them put together, is the third or "great
central platform," which attains an elevation
of about 70 feet, and covers an area of 60
acres. Here must have been the main city.
Further eastward are various irregular groups
of ruins, and one extensive platform of com-

paratively low elevation, which probably con-
stituted a sort of suburb, and was inhabited
by the poorer classes.

There is reason to believe that Susa was
already the capital in the time of Chedorlaomer.   A late Assyrian king declares that,
on his capture of the city (about B.C. 645), he
recovered from it a statue of Nana, which
Kudur-Nakhunta, an Elamitic monarch, had
carried off from Erech, in Babylonia, 1635
years previously.[1]   Kudur-Nakhunta must
thus have reigned about B.C. 2280, which
would be anterior to the time of Abraham,
who cannot be placed earlier than B.C. 2000.
Chedorlaomer may have been a monarch of
the same dynasty, who inherited Kudur-Nakhunta's suzerainty over Babylonia, and pushed
his conquests further.   The Susa of his time
was built probably of brick, and did not pos-
sess the architectural magnificence afterwards
conferred upon it by the Persian kings (Esther
i. 5, 6); but it looked down on meadows as
verdant as those of to-day ; it was embosomed

---

[1] G. Smith, " History of Asshur-bani-pal," pp. 234, 251, 254.

probably in even more abundant date-groves ; [1]
it had already, no doubt, its citadel and its
palace. The monarch from his lofty palace
mound commanded a view almost unexam-
pled for luxuriance and beauty. Gardens and
orchards clustered round the town and suburbs ;
beyond was the rolling plain, here spread out
in rich pastures, there covered by golden seas
of corn ; towards the south was the low range
of hills which stretches from Ahwaz westward ;
finally, towards the north were the limestone
ranges and snow-capped mountains of Luristan.
Invigorating breezes from the lofty mountain-
tops blew around him, tempering the sun's
heat and making music in the feathery palms ;
the verdure of konars, acacias, poplars, tama-
risks refreshed the eye ; the sound and sight
of gushing waters gratified both eye and ear ;
even the sense of smell was not unsatisfied, for
the rich vegetation of the verdant plains of
Shush is "interspersed with plants of a sweet-
scented and delicate iris" (*Iris Sisyrinchium*) [2]

[1] A sculptured slab of the time of Asshur-bani-pal shows the city
of Susa surrounded with date palms (Layard, "Monuments of
Nineveh," second series, pl. 49).

[2] Loftus, "Chaldæa and Susiana," p. 346.

—the " lily," according to some, from which Susa derived its name.

If the monarch needed some higher excitement than could be afforded by contemplation of the tranquil beauties of nature, he might descend to the plain and indulge himself in the delights of the chase. The king of beasts has always made his lair in many parts of the Susianian lowland, haunting especially the jungle along the banks of rivers, or the thickets of reeds upon the skirts of marshes. Francolins and rock partridges might test the royal sportsman's skill with the bow ;[1] and the wild ass, which in ancient times frequented portions of the country,[2] would try to the uttermost the speed and stoutness of the royal horses and the royal gaze-hounds. The actual occupations of the Susianian monarchs are not known to us, but we can scarcely doubt that they indulged in the same pastimes as their brother kings of Assyria and Babylonia, with whom the chase was a passion.

[1] The Assyrian sculptors represent birds as transfixed by the arrows of sportsmen (" Ancient Monarchies," vol. i. p. 287).
[2] " History of Asshur-bani-pal," p. 234.

After Elam had lost its independence, Susa increased in importance and architectural splendour, being chosen for their principal residence by the Achæmenian line of Persian monarchs. Though Cyrus was certainly not by descent an Elamite, yet it was as king of Elam that he commenced his conquests,[1] and a special affection for Elam may be traced among his successors. Darius, the son of Hystaspes, and cousin of Cyrus, appears to have been the first to make Susa the Persian capital. He fixed his ordinary abode at the Elamitic town, and erected a palace on the northern mound, which seems to have rivalled the splendour of the principal building at Persepolis. It was a pillared edifice, consisting of no less than seventy-two stone columns, disposed in four groups. A central phalanx of thirty-six columns, arranged in six rows of six each, supported probably a solid roof, and formed a throne room or hall of audience, 144 feet each way, open to the winds of heaven on all sides, but protected

---

[1] See the Nabonidus tablet, col. ii. line 1 ("Transactions of Bibl. Archæolog. Society," vol. vii. p. 155).

by the roof from sun and rain. On three sides of this great hall, distant from it about 64 feet, were detached groups of twelve columns each, arranged in two rows, and forming porticoes or colonnades, which may have been either *salles d'attente*, or resting-places for the royal guards, who would have had to be in attendance when the monarch granted audiences. The columns were of the Persepolitan type, with bell-shaped bases and complicated capitals,[1] crowned by two demibulls placed back to back, and attaining an elevation probably of between 60 and 70 feet.[2] Beneath them was a pavement of many-coloured marble or stone, red, and blue, and white, and black (Esther i. 6); and around were curtains, or hangings, white and green and blue, attached to the pillars by silver rings, and raised or lowered by the help of cords, which were purple and white (ib.) The palace had a frontage of 343 feet 9

---

[1] Loftus, "Chaldæa and Susiana," pp. 366–371.

[2] The tallest of the pillars now standing at Persepolis is 67 feet 4 inches (ib. p. 369, note). The palace at Susa is so nearly on the same plan as the Persepolitan, that its columns must be regarded as having had almost certainly the same height.

inches, with a depth of 244 feet.[1] It faced
to the north-east, courting the cool airs from
the Bakhtiyari mountains, and avoiding as
much as possible the glare of the sun's rays.
Around, on the broad space between the palace
and the edge of the platform, were courts and
gardens (Esther iv. 11, vii. 7), the latter perhaps diversified by fountains, water being raised
for the purpose, as at Babylon,[2] from the river
below. Here, during the spring-time, the Persian monarch enjoyed the delicious climate
of the upper Susianian plain, looking forth
from the deep shade of his pillared hall over
gardens and orchards, corn-fields and prairies
adorned with the brightest flowers, to the
snow-clad mountains of the far north-east, and
inhaling the soft fragrant breeze which came
laden with the scent of flowers from the rich
plain at the mountains' base. Here, when
evening drew on, the tables were spread and
the couches arranged for the banquets in which
the Achæmenian kings delighted to indulge
—an Ahasuerus (Xerxes) made a feast for
seven days to all the nobles gathered together

---

[1] Loftus, p. 367.   [2] Diod. Sic. ii. 10, § 5.

in Shushan in the court of the garden of the king's palace, while a Vashti made a feast for the women in the royal house (ib. i. 5, 9) ; or an Artaxerxes, seated by the side of his royal consort, took the wine-cup from the hand of his sad cup-bearer, and invited him to unfold his griefs (Neh. ii. 1–6).

The special river of Susa is called by Herodotus the Choaspes,[1] but by Daniel,[2] and in the Assyrian records,[3] the Ulai. The Ulai can scarcely be other than the Greek Eulæus, which the Greek geographers describe as a large stream east of the Choaspes,[4] and which has been generally identified with the Kuran. All accounts agree that Susa was on a large river—one that was navigable ; but at present the only stream that washes the ruins is the Shapur, which is little more than a rivulet. The difficulties seemed insuperable until it was found that the Kerkhah, which all agree to be the Choaspes, once bifurcated at Pai Pal,

---

[1] Herod., i. 188, v. 49, 52.   [2] Dan. viii. 2, 16.

[3] "Annals of Sennacherib," quoted by Layard in his "Nineveh and Babylon," p. 146 ; "History of Asshur-bani-pal," p. 198, line 9.

[4] Marc. Heracl. p. 18 ; Arrian, *Exp. Alex.*, vii. 7 ; Strabo, xv. 3, § 22 ; Ptol., *Geograph.*, vi. 3.

flowing from that point in two channels, one (the western) that in which it flows at present, and the other (the eastern) passing close to Susa, absorbing the Shapur, and joining the Kuran a little above Ahwaz.[1] It was this stream which the Assyrians called "Ulai," and the Greeks "Eulæus." As being, however, a branch of the Choaspes, it sometimes took that name ; and as flowing into the Kuran, it sometimes gave name to the lower course of that river. Its old bed may still be seen near the ruins of Susa, where its width is not less than 300 feet, and its depth, though it is much filled up with drifted sand, from 12 feet to 20.[2] The Arabs of the neighbourhood call it the *Shat atik*, or "ancient river," and the numerous remains of irrigating canals, with high embankments, on either side of it, show that it once carried a considerable body of water. Hence we may understand the expression of the Assyrian scribe in the annals of Asshur-bani-pal—"The Ulai *in its depth, a flood*, he crossed." The water of the stream

---

[1] Loftus, "Chaldæa and Susiana," pp. 423-430.
[2] Loftus, p. 424.

was light and agreeable to the taste ; it was also reckoned especially healthy ; and on account of these various good qualities, a sufficient quantity of it to supply the needs of the monarch accompanied all royal expeditions.[1]

[1] Herod., i. 188 ; Ctesias, "Persica," Fr. 49.

V.

SITES CONNECTED WITH THE HISTORY OF ABRAHAM, HARRAN, DAMASCUS, HEBRON.

THAT the Haran of Genesis (chap. xi. 31, 32, xii. 4, &c.), called Charran by the Septuagint, and by St. Stephen in the Acts of the Apostles (chap. vii. 2), is the Mesopotamian city known to the Greeks and Romans as Carrhæ, and still called (simply) HARRAN, is scarcely open to question. Haran was " beyond the river " from Palestine (Gen. xxxi. 21) ; it was in Padan-Aram, or Aram-Naharaim, both of them names attached by the Hebrews to the upper portion of the country which lies between the Tigris and Euphrates. The fancy that the Haran, which was the resting-place of Abraham and his family between their residence at " Ur of the Chaldees " and their settlement in Palestine, is to be identified with the small village near Damascus called at the present

F

time *Harran-el-Awamid*, though cherished by so acute a person as the late Dr. Beke,[1] is one hardly deserving of serious consideration. No traditions connect Abraham with this place. No evidence can be produced of the antiquity of the name at the site. It is on the wrong side of the Euphrates. It is remote from Gozan and Rezeph, which are connected with Haran in 2 Kings xix. 12 and Isa. xxxvii. 12, and from Halah and Habor, which are connected with it in 1 Chron. v. 26. It is altogether an insignificant locality, unknown until the time when Dr. Beke made discovery of it, and unnoticed by any ancient historian or geographer, Greek, Roman, or Assyrian. The Mesopotamian Haran, or Harran on the contrary, is one of the most noted towns of Western Asia, and one which appears repeatedly in history from the time of Abraham to A.D. 1200.

Harran lies on the river Belik, which is an affluent of the Euphrates, about twenty miles south-east of Orfah, and seventy from the

---

[1] *Athenæum* of November 23, 1861 ; February 1, 15 ; March 1, 29 ; and May 24, 1862.

point where the Belik forms its junction with the great Mesopotamian river. It is abundantly supplied with water, both from the Belik itself and from a number of springs. The country in the neighbourhood is undulating, and in places clothed with wood,[1] but on the whole may be regarded as best adapted for pasture. Haran was also well situated for purposes of commerce. A caravan route between the east and west passed through it on the way to cross the middle Euphrates, at the ford known as Zeugma,[2] and another probably struck it from the south, and was continued to Amida or Diarbekr. These lines seem to correspond with the two " Royal Roads " mentioned by Ammianus,[3] one of which took a south-east direction by way of Adiabêné and the Tigris, while the other inclined to the south-west by way of Assyria and the Euphrates. The natural products which the Haranites would have to exchange with their neighbours were wine, pistachio nuts, corn,

[1] *Dio Cass.*, xl. 21.

[2] This route is indicated in Ezek. xxvii. 23. Compare Ritter, *Erdkunde*, vol. vii. p. 296.

[3] *Amm. Marc.*, xxiii. 3.

and wool, perhaps certain metals. They would import the manufactures of Babylon, the horses and mules of Armenia, and the varied goods which Phœnicia collected from Africa and Europe.

Abraham's sojourn at Haran does not appear to have been long. He was there, not as a merchant, or as a permanent settler, but simply as a member of a wandering pastoral tribe, which needed a good grazing ground for its flocks and herds. The site was suitable for the purpose; but it was perhaps scarcely sufficient for the sustenance of the very considerable body of nomads, which had quitted Southern Chaldæa on a divine summons, or under an impulse of restlessness, and had wandered northwards. Abraham, after a brief stay, determined on a further movement. The tribe, it is probable, was cramped for room. The divine purpose, which had at any rate underlain the emigration, was not satisfied. A distinct intimation of the will of God caused Abraham to start forth afresh. He "took Sarai his wife, and Lot his brother's son, and all their substance that they had gathered, and the souls that they had gotten in Haran ; and they went forth to go into the land of Canaan ; and into the land of Canaan they came " (Gen. xii. 5).

But on the way to Canaan there is reason to believe that they made a halt at DAMASCUS. Damascus is of all the cities of the world the one which has the longest continuous history. Not so ancient as Babylon, or Memphis, or Ur, or Susa, or This (Teni), she has remained a city from the time of her first appearance on the world's stage, without break or interruption. She has a continuous history of almost four thousand years. Abraham's connection with Damascus appears in Scripture from two, and two only, notices. The " steward of his house " was " Eliezer of Damascus " (Gen. xv. 2) ; and when he hung upon the rear of Chedorlaomer's army, defeated a detachment of the army, and recovered his nephew Lot, he pursued the retreating invaders to a town in the near neighbourhood of that city (ibid., xiv. 15). Profane history and existing tradition confirm and enlarge the scriptural indications ;

but, as usual in such cases, add features which are questionable, or worse than questionable. Nicolas of Damascus says that Abraham, having settled at Damascus, "was made king of the place,"[1] which is exceedingly improbable; while a modern tale, which claims to be traditional, makes him reside during his stay in the Damascene oasis at Birzeh, three miles north of Damascus, but discredits itself by making Birzeh not only his residence, but the place of his birth.[2] An earlier Mohammedan account declares that at Birzeh "Abraham worshipped God on his return from the pursuit of the kings who had plundered Sodom, and carried away Lot."[3] It is certain that there is at Birzeh a chapel to Abraham (*Makam Ibrahim*), which is regarded as possessing a high degree of sanctity, and is a place whereto pilgrimages are made at a certain season every year. Josephus[4] and Justin[5] may be added to the number of those

---

[1] Nic. Dam. Fr. 30.

[2] Porter, "Five Years in Damascus," vol. i. p. 82 ; Robson in "Stanley's Lectures on the Jewish Church," vol. i. p. 486.

[3] Ibn 'Asâker, quoted by Porter, *l.c.*

[4] Joseph., *Ant. Jud.*, i. 7, § 2.

[5] Justin, *Hist. Philipp.*, xxxvi. 2.

who regard Abraham's sojourn at Damascus as a fact.

Damascus undoubtedly lies on the way that an emigrant would naturally take who left Harran to settle in Canaan. Abraham, on reaching it, would naturally have made it a resting-place. There is no spot on the earth's surface more attractive, more luxuriant, more lovely, more delicious. A broad plain, stretching from the south-eastern base of Antilibanus towards the Syrian desert, is watered by a number of smaller rivulets, and by one " deep, broad, rushing mountain river."[1] This abundant stream creates a region of extraordinary fertility. The Damascene plain is estimated to cover a space not much short of 240 square miles.[2] It is everywhere covered with the richest vegetation. "The natural soil is a sandy loam, not promising any very great fertility. But the growth and decay of many thousand years have enriched it" (and must have enriched it before the historical period) "with a thick layer of vegetable mould, which has

[1] Robinson, " Later Researches in Palestine," p. 446.
[2] Porter, " Five Years in Damascus," vol. i. p. 26.

productive qualities that appear to be inexhaustible. With scant labour and with no artificial dressing, heavy crops are produced of almost every kind; and the land seems equally fitted for the growth of grain, fruit, and flowers, for corn-fields, orchards, vineyards, olive-grounds, kitchen gardens, and flower-gardens. In the remoter parts of the plain all the various species of grain for the use of man or beast are raised in profusion.[1] Besides these, tobacco, cotton, hemp, madder, ricinus, are successfully cultivated. Vegetables of all kinds are grown, and are abundant and cheap.[2] Of forest trees, the principal are the palm, the plane, and the poplar. Planes grow to a great size; there is one within the bounds of the modern city, the stem of which measures forty feet in circumference. But the glory of the plain consists in its orchards and gardens, which extend for miles, and form a wilderness of scented verdure. Lemons, oranges, and citrons, bearing fruit and flowers at once, delight the eye with their bright green foliage and their golden

[1] Robinson, *l. c.*   [2] Ibid., p. 452.

produce, while they fill the air with a delicious perfume that is sometimes almost overpowering.[1] Great apricot trees are laden and bent down under strings of ripe, luscious fruit. The blue haze of the olive contrasts well with the livelier verdure of the fig and walnut. Mulberries, vines, quinces, peaches, pear-trees, apple-trees, pistachios, almonds, hazels, plums, prunes, flourish on all sides, and for the most part bear abundantly, while beneath their shade the pomegranate and the oleander brighten the scene with their delicate blossoms. Damascus lies embosomed in a sea of varied foliage, resting, like an island of Paradise,[2] in the green enclosure of its beautiful gardens."[3]

If the extreme luxuriance and the immense productiveness which now astonish the traveller who visits the Damascene oasis, arising as they do in great part from the labour and skill of man during four thousand years, did not present themselves in their present guise

---

[1] Tristram's " Land of Israel," p. 611.

[2] Conybeare and Howson, "Life and Epistles of St. Paul," p. 470.

[3] See "St. Paul in Damascus and Arabia," pp. 12, 13.

to the early wanderers who had accompanied Abraham in his movement southwards from Harran, still in its mere natural condition, with little or no aid from man, the Ghûtah (as it is now called) must have been a " Paradise ; " and a body of weary wayfarers could not but have stopped there, attracted by its manifold beauties and delights and conveniences, if the line of their march conducted them to the neighbourhood. But though attracted, and for a while detained by natural beauties and advantages which were almost without a parallel, such a company as that which Abraham led would scarcely have been satisfied to select the spot for their permanent abode, or even to remain very long encamped there. The wealth of the Hebrews was in their flocks and herds, which consisted especially of sheep and goats. These would only flourish and multiply on a drier soil, in a more bracing air, browsing a scantier and less succulent herbage than that which springs in the meadows watered by the Barada and its sister streams. The rank lush growth of the Ghûtah would in a short time have been fatal to them.

Abraham, therefore, and the band that followed him, made (we may be sure) no long stay in the Damascene oasis, but after a short sojourn struck their tents, and once more marched southwards towards the "land of promise."

May it be permitted us here to pause a moment and contemplate the stirring scene? A late charming writer has observed that the "unchanged habits of the East render it a kind of living Pompeii. The outward appearances, which in the case of the Greeks and Romans we know only through art and writing, through marble, fresco, and parchment, in the case of Jewish history we know through the forms of actual men, living and moving before us, wearing almost the same garb, speaking in almost the same language, and certainly with the same turns of speech and tones and manners."[1] The start of a caravan at the present day on a migration or a pilgrimage will furnish a lively image of the departure from Damascus of Abraham and his followers. The multitude of men and

[1] Dean Stanley, "Lectures on the Jewish Church," vol. i. p. 11.

women and children and beasts would be collected together in some open space without the walls of the town. All the substance whereof they were possessed would be " heaped high on the backs of their kneeling camels. The ' slaves that they had bought in Haran ' would be running along by their sides. Round about them are their flocks of sheep and goats, and the asses moving underneath the towering forms of the camels. The chief is there amidst the stir of movement, or resting at noon within his black tent, marked out from the rest by his cloak of brilliant scarlet, by the fillet of rope which binds the loose handkerchief round his head, by the spear which he holds in his hand to guide the march and to fix the encampment. The chief's wife, the princess (Sarah) of the tribe, is there in her own tent to make the cakes and prepare the usual meal of milk and butter ; the slave or the child is ready to bring in the red lentil soup for the weary hunter or to kill the calf for the unexpected guest." [1] All is bustle and expectation. The loads are

[1] Dean Stanley's " Lectures on the Jewish Church," vol. i. pp. 11, 12.

fixed ; the camels groan, and make a pretence of not being able to rise ; the drivers shout, and shriek, and belabour the beasts with their staves ; the asses bray ; the children scream ; the chief gives his last orders ; the leading camel steps forth, and the march is begun.

Abraham's movements in Palestine appear for a time to have been desultory and without fixed object. He encamped for a while at She-chem (Gen. xii. 6), and again at Bethel (ib. x. 3) ; but the place where he finally settled was Hebron. "Abram removed his tent, and came and dwelt in the plain (oak-wood ?) of Mamre, which is in Hebron, and built there an altar unto the Lord" (ib. xiii. 18). The Palestinian high land south of Jerusalem has a general elevation of from 2000 to 3000 feet. It is supplied with water chiefly by wells, and by the winter rains, which are collected into reservoirs, whence the necessary fluid is drawn during the remainder of the year. Very little of it is now wooded, but anciently it would appear that in places there were ilex or tere-binth groves, which spread a welcome shade over certain districts. The land generally was, however, unsheltered by trees, open, bare mostly of natural produce, but capable of cultivation, and productive, through expenditure of human labour, of corn, wine, and oil in considerable quantities. But the district was especially suited for pasturage. The tract between Hebron and Jerusalem is for the most part a level tableland, covered in the springtime with a short but nutritious grass, and in many places with a carpet of brilliant flowers,[1] dreary and desolate-looking during the remainder of the year, yet still yielding sufficient herbage for the sustenance of considerable flocks of sheep and goats. " West and north-west of the highlands, where the sea-breezes are felt, there is considerably more vegetation. The Wady-es-Sunt derives its name from the acacias which line its sides. In the same neighbourhood olives abound, and give the country almost a wooded appearance. The dark, grateful foliage of the *butm*, or terebinth, is frequent; and one of these trees, perhaps the largest in Palestine, stands a few minutes' ride from the ancient Socho. About ten miles

---

[1] See Dean Stanley's " Sinai and Palestine," p. 139.

north of this, near the site of the ancient Kir-jath-Jearim—the 'city of forests'—are some thickets of pine and laurel, which Tobler compares with European woods."

Hebron lies east of the ridge which forms the backbone of Southern Palestine, in a valley which runs towards the south-east. The valley is at first wide and open, possesses at any rate one " very large and beautiful oak-tree (*Quercus ilex*)," and is cultivated in corn (*durra*) and vineyards.[1] As it approaches the town the valley narrows and deepens ; a portion of it is " thickly covered with olive orchards of very old trees,"[2] but the town itself occupies the whole valley for some space, extending across it and spreading also over the lower portion of the declivity of the hills on either side. The main town is on the slope of the eastern hill, and consequently looking west ; it is clustered about the chief object of interest in the place, the massive building containing the tombs of the patriarchs, presently to be described, now the principal mosque of the

---

[1] Robinson, " Biblical Researches in Palestine," vol. ii. pp. 428, 429. [2] Ibid., p. 432.

city. Above and below the town, where it occupies the valley, are two reservoirs, kept supplied by the rains, on which the inhabitants depend mainly for their water supply. The larger of the two is towards the south. It is a square of 133 English feet each way, built with hewn stones of good workmanship, and 21 feet 8 inches deep. The northern pool is smaller; it measures 85 feet in length by 55 feet broad, and has a depth of 18 feet 8 inches.[1] Both reservoirs have every appearance of a high antiquity. Over one or the other David probably hung up the assassins of Ishbosheth (2 Sam. iv. 12). It is possible that they may have belonged to the old Kirjath-Arba (Josh. xiv. 15), and have existed in the time of Abraham.

The external appearance of the "sepulchral quadrangle" enclosing the tombs of the patriarchs, is best given by Dr. Robinson. "The exterior," he says,[2] "has the appearance of a long and lofty building in the form of a paral-

---

[1] See the careful description of Dr. Robinson in the above-mentioned work, vol. ii. pp. 432, 433.

[2] Ibid., pp. 434, 435.

lelogram, its longest dimension being along the valley from N.N.W. to S.S.E., and not as in most ancient churches from west to east. We measured on a line parallel to its eastern side and southern end as near as we could. . . . The length proved to be nearest 200 feet, and the breadth 115 feet. The height cannot be less than 50 or 60 feet. The walls are built of very large stones, all bevelled and hewn smooth, and similar in all respects to the most ancient parts of the walls around the Haram at Jerusalem. But they are not in general so large, nor is the bevelling so deep. The architecture has this peculiarity, that the walls are built up externally with square pilasters, sixteen on each side and eight at each end, without capitals, except a sort of cornice which extends along the whole building. Above this the walls have been raised by the Muslims 8 or 10 feet higher, with a small turret or minaret at each corner.[1] The places of entrance are at the two northern (western ?) corners, where a long and broad

[1] This is a mistake. Only two of the corners, those at the north-west and south-east angles, are crowned by minarets (Stanley, "Jewish Church," vol. i. p. 403, and plan opposite p. 499).

flight of steps, built up and covered along each side of the building externally, leads to a door opening into the court within." Dr. Robinson should have added that the level line of the enclosing wall is broken to the eye, not only by the minarets at the corners, but also by the roof of the mosque, which shows above it, revealing even the upper portion of its windows.

The interior of the building became first known to the present generation through the visit which His Royal Highness the Prince of Wales paid to Hebron in the year 1862. The Prince and his suite were conducted up the south-eastern staircase to the platform on which the mosque and other buildings containing the tombs stand. Passing through two empty rooms at the top of the stairs, they entered a court or area, which occupies about one-fourth of the enclosed space. The outer wall of the enclosure rose on their right hand, but was raised above the pavement of the court only a few feet. On the remaining three sides the court was enclosed by buildings. To the north, opposite them, was a long lofty room leading to two circular chambers, which contained coffin-like monuments, surrounded by an iron railing, and regarded respectively as the tombs or shrines of Jacob and Leah. On the left was another long and lofty room, skirting the western wall of the enclosure, and leading to a domed chamber attached to the enclosure on the outside and projecting from it, lighted by painted windows, and regarded as the tomb of Joseph. Fronting the northern chamber and the shrines of Jacob and Leah, and forming the southern boundary of the court, was a cloister of three round arches, covered in by three domed roofs, and forming an outer *narthex*, which opened into an inner one of the same size, having an empty chamber in the middle, and to right and left the tombs or shrines of Abraham and Sarah, each guarded by silver gates, and adorned with hangings or carpets. From this double portico the mosque proper was entered. This was a square edifice, supported on four central pillars equally spaced, and thus divided into a nave and two aisles, the nave being completely open, but the aisles containing respectively, midway in their length, the shrines of Isaac and Rebekah, that of Isaac on the right hand towards the west, that of Rebekah exactly opposite, on the left hand towards the east. The mosque, including the porch, occupies rather more than a third of the entire enclosed space. It is manifestly a Byzantine Church transformed into a mosque, and probably dates from the time of Constantine. The outer wall, however, which is of a marble-like stone, highly polished, and composed of huge blocks bevelled at their edges, is pronounced to be certainly Jewish,[1] and thought to date from about B.C. 1000.

There seem to be sufficient grounds for believing that the original structure was raised for the purpose of enclosing and protecting the portion of the eastern Hebron hill which contained "the cave of Macpelah." The belief on the spot is, that underneath the pavement of the mosque and the court attached to it is a large double cave, in which are the actual burial-places of the patriarchal seven—Abraham, Isaac, Jacob, Joseph, Sarah,

[1] Stanley, "Jewish Church," vol. i. p. 498 ; Robinson, "Biblical Researches," vol. i. p. 436.

Rebekah, Leah, situated as indicated by their respective cenotaphs above. Into this cavern there are at present no means of entering. One aperture alone, circular, and no more than 8 inches in diameter, opens from the pavement of the mosque into the dark void beneath. It is close to the south-east corner of the shrine of Abraham, and was thought by the Prince of Wales' party, who were allowed to feel it with their hands,[1] to be an actual hole in the living rock. The gloom of the cave was such that they could see nothing of its contents. At night, it is said, a lamp is let down by a chain, and burns upon the tomb of the great patriarch till morning, when it is drawn up; but the party accompanying the Prince, whose visit was in the daytime, could not prevail upon the guardians of the mosque to let down the lamp.

The most sceptical can scarcely doubt that six at any rate of the tombs guarded with such jealous care, and protected by a massive structure dating probably from B.C. 1000, are genuine—the real tombs of the six persons

---

[1] Stanley, p. 504.

declared by Scripture [1] to have been interred in the cave of Macpelah, at Hebron, in the land of Canaan. With respect to the tomb of Joseph there is some uncertainty. That he was originally buried at Shechem appears from Josh. xxiv. 32; but it is certainly possible, and perhaps not improbable, that his remains were at a later date transferred from Shechem to Hebron, and there found their final resting-place.[2]

---

[1] See Gen. xxiii. 19, xxv. 9, xlix. 31, l. 13.

[2] Joseph., *Ant. Jud.*, ii. 8, § 2; Acts vii. 15, 16; Stanley, "Jewish Church," vol. i. p. 502.

VI.

EGYPTIAN SITES—ZOAN AND PITHOM.

THE first Biblical mention of Zoan is in Num. xiii. 22, where it appears as an ancient and well-known city. "Hebron," we are told, " was built seven years before Zoan in Egypt." It is next heard of in the 78th Psalm, which is ascribed to Asaph, and which appears at any rate to belong to David's time. There " the field (*saddeh*) of Zoan" appears as the place in which the miracles of Moses were wrought (vers. 12, 43). In Isa. xxx. 4 we find that the ambassadors whom Hezekiah sent to implore the assistance of the king of Egypt when he was expecting to be attacked by Sennacherib went to Zoan and Hanes. These are the chief scriptural notices of Zoan.[1] What can be gathered from them ?

[1] The name of Zoan is coupled with that of Noph in Isa. xix. 13, and occurs also among the cities of Egypt in Ezek. xxx. 14, but these passages give no indication of locality.

First, it is clear that Zoan was a very ancient city. Hebron was an old city in the days of Abraham. It had been originally built by the Anakim, a people of huge stature who belong to very primitive times (Num. xiii. 33 ; Josh. xiv. 15), and had been called by them Kiriath-Arba, after one of their chiefs. Zoan was nearly contemporaneous with it, and must therefore be assigned an almost equal antiquity.

Secondly, it was probably the capital city of the Pharaoh of the Exodus. That city is not named in the narrative of Moses ; but as there is no reason to doubt the tradition that the scene of the Mosaic miracles was "the field of Zoan," and as they were certainly performed in the vicinity of a city which was the residence of the monarch of the time, the inference is almost a necessary one, that Zoan was either the Pharaoh's only capital, or at any rate one of his capitals. The continued residence of the king at the place during an entire year, which is implied in the narrative, is in favour of its being his sole capital.

Thirdly, the city of the Pharaoh of the

Exodus, presumably Zoan, was situated on the Nile, or on some recognised branch of it. The use of the expression, "the river" (*han-nahar*), in Exod. vii. 15–24, is conclusive on this point. In an Egyptian narrative "the river" can only be the Nile, as in a Syrian one it can only be the Euphrates.

Fourthly, Zoan must have been situated low down the Nile, in or near the Delta, and towards its more eastern parts. All the geographical sites connected with the residence of the Israelites in Egypt—Goshen, Rameses, Pithom, Succoth, Pi-hahiroth, Migdol—belong to the eastern side of the country, and either to the Delta itself or to the tract adjoining the Delta towards the east.

Now, in the situation thus indicated is found a town of great antiquity, which the Egyptians called " Zal " or " Zan," the Greeks Tan-is, and which to this day bears the name of " San." It lies upon that branch of the Nile which the Greeks named after it, " the Tanitic," and it was the capital of Menephthah, son and successor of Rameses II., who is almost certainly the Pharaoh of the Exodus.

These circumstances, and the fact that the
LXX. interpreters replace the Hebrew "Zoan"
by "Tanis" in every place where it occurs,
sufficiently explain and justify the identification of the Hebrew "Zoan" with the
modern "San," which is now made by almost
all comparative geographers.

San or Zoan is situated in what is now a
most desolate region.   "The vast monotonous
plain of the Delta is broken," says Mr. R. S.
Poole, "when we see on the horizon the lofty
mounds of Zoan.   All around is desolation.
When the Nile has spread over the land
marsh plants spring up, and there are scanty
patches of vegetation to point a contrast;
but the dry season withers all, and then the
whole tract is one brown space of desolate
sameness.   A few date-sellers may cross the
mound, and that is all the commerce.   Arabs
of the western desert here chase the gazelle
with falcon and greyhound.   No description
need emphasize these few words.   *There is
indeed no scenery to describe;* one vast silent
solitude, without variety of form or colour,
a weary wilderness; all the sadder when we

think that the hard soil beneath our feet would yield a triple harvest, if war and neglect and tyranny had not depopulated and then marred the land."[1]

But perhaps there is no place in the world where the contrast between what is and what was is, to an instructed mind, more striking. When Moses trod the streets of Zoan, or stood by its river's brink to meet the great king as he went forth to the water in the morning (Exod. vii. 15), or stretched forth his rod over the green fields in its vicinity (ib. ix. 22, 23), instead of a "weary wilderness," a "vast silent solitude," a "brown space of desolate sameness," the whole scene was one of life, of motion, of bright colour, of almost endless variety. Here, where are now the lofty arid mounds, was the city with its stirring life, its noise, its traffic, its confusion. Westward stood the great temple originally built by the "shepherd king," Apepi, to his god Set, or Sutech, and recently repaired, or rather perhaps rebuilt, by Rameses-Miamun with pink granite, conveyed a distance of 700 miles

---

[1] See his "Cities of Egypt," pp. 84, 85.

from the quarries of Syêné, and boasting at
least fourteen graceful obelisks.   Eastward
stood another temple, wholly the construction
of Rameses, less extensive than the other, but
of equally rich and varied workmanship.   The
outer temple walls were adorned with reliefs
on a gigantic scale, coloured with brilliant
hues, showing forth the great conqueror's wars
in Asia.   The inner courts were surrounded
with corridors of pillars, and exhibited the
forms of gods and goddesses receiving worship and offerings.   Troops of priests paraded
the courts and halls, here offering incense,
there sacrifice, or marching in solemn pro-
cession, singing hymns to the music of flutes
and pipes, of cymbals and harps and drums.
The streets of the town were astir with busy
crowds, bent on traffic or on pleasure.   Brown
Egyptians, red Arabs from the Yemen, stal-
wart blacks from the Soudan, pale blue-eyed
Libyans from the North-African coast, down-
trodden Israelites bearing their tale of bricks,
jostled each other in the broader thorough-
fares, whence they had to remove into the
side lanes or to take refuge in corners when

the great noble, borne in his palanquin by his domestic slaves, or the young dandy, driving his pair-horse chariot, claimed a passage that it would have been rash to refuse.

Outside the town was the river, navigable from the sea, and crowded with ships and boats. Here glided arks containing images of the gods; there hurried on the galley of a grandee, with its sail set, and impelled besides by forty or fifty rowers; heavy merchantmen floated down the stream, or were towed up from the shore; light skiffs of the papyrus plant—" vessels of bulrushes "[1] —darted in and out of the shipping in all directions. From the river on either side branched out canals, which contained fish of various kinds, and conveyed the Nile water far and wide over the soil that is now so parched and arid. The land about the town —" the field of Zoan "—everywhere bore grain, or fruit, or vegetables. The city is described by an Egyptian writer of the time of Rameses II. as " pleasant to live in." " Its

---

[1] Isa, xviii. 2.

fields," he says, "are full of good things, and life passes in constant plenty and abundance. The canals are rich in fish; the lakes swarm with birds; the meadows are green with vegetables; there is no end of the lentils; melons with a taste like honey grow in the irrigated gardens. The barns are full of wheat and *durra*, and reach as high as heaven. Onions and grapes grow in the enclosures, and the apple-tree blooms among them. The vine, the almond-tree, and the fig-tree are found in the orchards. Sweet is their wine for the inhabitants of Kemi (Egypt); they mix it with honey. The red fish is common in the lotus canal, the bori fish in the ponds; many varieties of the same, together with carp and pike, are in the canal of Pu-harotha; fat fish and *khipti-pennu* fish are to be found in the pools of the inundation; the *hauaz* fish in the full mouth of the Nile, near the city of the conqueror. The city canal Pshenhor produces salt, the lake region of Pahir-natron. Sea-going ships enter the harbour; plenty and abundance are perpetual."[1] From the Book of Exodus we learn[2] that among the crops produced in the neighbourhood were not only "wheat and rye" (*i.e.*, *durra*), but also "barley and flax." In spring and early summer the "field of Zoan" must have presented a glorious spectacle; even at other seasons it was probably a pleasant sight, since, when the land in the Delta is well cultivated, it readily bears "a triple harvest."

At the same time it must be admitted that in Egypt there is always, under all circumstances, a certain tameness and uniformity. Either the inundation covers the whole country, leaving nothing to be seen but a wide waste of waters, and the scattered towns and villages perched here and there on their artificial elevations in its midst; or else there is a uniformity of greenness when the crops are springing up, or a uniformity of yellow ripeness when they are nearly ready for the sickle, or a uniformity of brown dreariness

---

[1] See the "Letter of Panbesa," translated by Mr. Goodwin in "Records of the Past," vol. vi. pp. 13–16, and by Dr. Brugsch in his *Geschichte Ægyptens*, pp. 547, 548.

[2] Exod. ix. 31, 32.

when they have been cut. The absence of hill and dale, of woodland, or down, or moor, of mountain heights and mountain streams, and bubbling rills, and hanging copses, and leafy glades; and again the uniformity of sky, changeless blue for the most part day after day for months together—produce an impression of dull monotony, so far as nature is concerned, and explain the longing that man has ever felt in Egypt to break the uniformity by daring attempts, extraordinary freaks, in building and excavating, in piling pyramids, and carving rocks into colossi, and rearing obelisks, and cutting canals, and making labyrinths, and in every way running counter to the nature that is so dull, so tame, so without variety. At Zoan a grand effect was produced by the height of the great mound, of the temples which crowned it, and of the obelisks which rose like spires above the level lines of the temple roofs, pointing to the heaven above them.

Pithom is mentioned once only in the Bible (Exod. i. 11), and there in a connection which gives no certain indication of locality. All that we are told concerning it is that it was one of the " treasure-cities " (*'arey miske-nôth*) which the Israelites built for the Pharaoh who began their heavy oppression. The translation " treasure-cities " is disputed ; and it is certainly remarkable that the Septuagint interpreters, writing in Egypt, did not so understand the expression, but translated it by πόλεις ὀχυράς—" strong cities" or " fortified cities." Others have suggested the meaning of "store-cities " or " magazine-cities "—*i.e.*, places where arms and provisions were laid up in store ; and recently Professor Lansing has in a Review article [1] proposed the rendering of " residence-cities," or places at which the Court sometimes took up its abode. All the translations, except the last, would point to a place on or near the frontier, and considering the part of Egypt in which the Israelites were located, on or near the north-eastern frontier, where it is certain that about the time of Rameses II. great efforts were made to strengthen the defences of the empire,

---

[1] See *Monthly Interpreter* for November 1885, p. 33.

H

and accumulate the means of resisting the advance of an enemy.[1]

Some further light is thrown on the situation of Pithom by a well-known passage of Herodotus.[2] The Hebrew "Pithom" would express the Egyptian "Pa-Tum," a city long known to have been built by Rameses II.; and "Pa-Tum" is exactly rendered by the Greek Πάτουμ-ος, which Herodotus places on the line of the ancient canal between the Nile and the Red Sea. This canal followed the course of the present Wady Toumilat, along which pass the modern fresh-water canal and the modern Cairo-Suez railway; and it had long been clear to scholars that Pithom would have to be sought along the line of this wady, though on which side of the ancient canal and at what particular point of the wady was uncertain. When, therefore, in 1883, excavations, conducted by M. Naville[3] on behalf of the

---

[1] Birch, "Egypt from the Earliest Times," p. 125.

[2] See Herod., ii. 158.

[3] For an account of the excavations, see M. Naville's "Store-City of Pithom," pp. 2–11, and plates. Earlier notices will be found in the *Academy* for February 24, March 3 and 17, and April 7 of 1883; and also in the *British Quarterly Review* for July of that year.

" Egyptian Exploration Fund" in the Wady Toumilat, laid bare the site of an ancient Egyptian city about twelve miles from Ismailia, on the southern bank of the present and the northern bank of the ancient canal, and the name of the city was shown by the monuments found in it to have been " Pa-Tum," the discovery was immediately hailed as fixing at once and for ever the *exact* position of the long-sought town, to which it had previously been only possible to approximate. If any doubt could have been entertained as to the decipherment of the name, it was set at rest by the simultaneous discovery, on the same site, of Roman fragments bearing the name of Ero or Heroöpolis,[1] since the identity of Pithom with Heroöpolis was scarcely doubted by comparative geographers.

Pithom, then, may be considered to be now definitely identified with the ruins at Tel-el-Maskoutah. They lie in the valley, through which pass the Cairo-Suez canal and railway, about twelve miles west of Ismailia, and about twenty miles east of Tel-el-Kebir. The chief

---

[1] See M. Naville's work, pl. 11.

remains are contained within a square enclosure, surrounded by a wall 8 yards thick
and about 235 yards long each way. This
enclosure is probably the ancient *temenos* of
the great temple of Tum, one of the Egyptian
sun-gods, which occupied its south-western
corner, and appears by inscriptions found on
the spot to have been built by Rameses II.
North of the temple M. Naville found a number of square chambers of different sizes, which
he believed to be " store-chambers " or grana-
ries, wherein the Pharaohs deposited the corn
needed for the food of their frontier troops
and garrisons ; but Professor Lansing says that
similar chambers are to be found in all the
Egyptian city mounds, and regards them as
essential parts of the mounds, which were built,
he thinks, in this way for the saving of material,
and for securing greater dryness to the mounds
and the buildings erected on them.[1] If this
be so, the evidence that Pithom was a " store-
city " fails ; though still it may have been one,
or, possibly, *'ir miskenoth* may have some other
quite different meaning.

[1] *Monthly Interpreter* for November 1885, pp. 39–50.

The present condition of the site of Pithom is not very unlike that of San, as described above. There is indeed rather more greenness in the immediate vicinity, since a branch canal conveys water to some of the low ground in the neighbourhood, which is cultivated in grain by the natives.[1] But, apart from this, the eye roams over much the same sort of dreary waste as that which surrounds the site of Tanis. The chief difference is that north and south of the wady are uplands of sandy soil, covered here and there with a coarse grass or with stunted bushes, which, as they could never have been irrigated, must always have presented much the same picture of desolation as they do at the present day.

Thus, even anciently, Pithom cannot have been very attractive or very beautiful. It had, no doubt, its gardens and its orchards; and a green line of growing crops may have extended from it, like a riband, eastward and westward along the course of the wady. But northward and southward the desert shuts it

---

[1] Naville, "Store-City of Pithom," plan of the city at the end of the volume.

closely in, frowning down upon it in bare and
dry sterility. Even the ancient Egyptians,
with all their laboriousness and all their engi-
neering skill, can scarcely have rendered these
arid tracts productive.

But Pithom, in the days of Rameses II.,
was undoubtedly a place of stir and bustle.
Along the canal passed continually the
heavily-laden vessels, which brought the
wares of Arabia and Ethiopia, and perhaps
of India, from the Red Sea and Indian
Ocean to the great Egyptian centres of Memphis, Tanis, and Heliopolis. The sailors
would go ashore at each important town
along their route, and arouse nocturnal echoes
with their songs and shoutings. Sometimes
a fleet of war vessels may have passed from
sea to sea, streamers flying, troops cheering,
and rowers labouring at their long sweeps.
Sometimes, no doubt, armies, on their march
into Asia, took the line of the wady, which was
the shortest from Memphis, Heliopolis, and
Upper Egypt to the main route through the
desert. The line of the canal was also,
probably, a line of land trade, which caravans

would have followed as they passed backwards and forwards between Syria and the great city of Memphis.

When we stand on the mound of Tel-el-Maskoutah and view the great massive wall, 940 yards long and 8 yards broad, which surrounds the enclosure, and which originally can scarcely have been less than 15 or 20 feet in height, and further contemplate the mound itself, which is a mass of brickwork, we see tangible evidence of that "service with rigour" which Israel was called on to undergo for more than eighty years at the hands of their Egyptian oppressors.[1] Not a brick in that wall, or in the excavated chambers, or in the entire mound, which covers a space of ten acres, but was probably modelled by Israelite hands, borne on Israelite backs, and placed in position by Israelites working under the lash of the "taskmaster." It has been said that the great works of Rameses-Miamun were for the most part cemented with blood.[2] Human nature shrinks from estimating the sum-total

---

[1] Exod. i. 11–14, ii. 11, v. 4–19.
[2] Lenormant, *Manuel d'Histoire Ancienne*, vol. i. p. 423.

of the suffering which a single wretched egotist caused his fellow-men to endure in the course of the sixty-seven years of his long and sanguinary reign.

It must have added to the misery of the down-trodden captives that they had to labour for a king who was not content with regarding himself as raised far above all the other dwellers upon earth, but claimed to be on a level with God. In the very temple with which Rameses II. crowned the platform of Tel-el-Maskoutah, he proclaimed this audacious assumption in the most open and unmistakable way. Right in front of the temple, at its entrance, on either side of the *dromos*, or paved pathway leading to the great gates, he caused to be placed a huge monolith, representing a group, of which his was the central figure.[1] On his right and on his left, in a less dignified position than his own, were Ra, the supreme sun-god, and Tum, the god of the place, the three thus challenging the worship of those who entered the temple, and Rameses putting himself before

---

[1] Naville, " Store-City of Pithom," pp. 1, 2.

the eyes of all as the chief object of adoration.
And this was an innovation on his part.
" Other kings," as I have elsewhere observed,[1]
"had arrogated to themselves a certain qualified
divinity, and after their deaths had sometimes
been placed by some of their successors on a
par with the real national gods.   It remained
for Rameses II. to associate himself during his
lifetime with such leading deities as Phthah,
Ammon, and Horus "—I might have added,
" as Ra and Tum "—" and to claim equally
with them the religious regards of his subjects."   The Tel-el-Maskoutah is an enduring
monument of his impiety ; for one of the
monoliths still stands in front of the temple,
and is the most conspicuous object on the
site.

[1] " History of Ancient Egypt," vol. ii. pp. 325, 326.

VII.

FURTHER EGYPTIAN SITES—MEMPHIS, THEBES, MIGDOL, SYENE.

THERE can be little doubt that Memphis is intended in some, at any rate, of the passages of Scripture, which speak of an Egyptian city, called Noph (Isa. xix. 13; Jer. ii. 16, xliv. 1, xlvi. 14, 19; Ezek. xxx. 13, 16, or Moph (Hos. ix. 6). The native name of Memphis was "Men-nefer," or "Men-nofer," out of which the Assyrians made "Mempi," the Greeks "Memphis," the Arabs "Menf," and the Hebrews, as it would seem, "Moph" or "Noph." Men-nofer meant "the good dwelling" or "the pleasant dwelling," and, according to the tradition, was the name given to the city by its founder, M'na or Menes. The situation is the best that Egypt offers for the site of a great city. Here is the junction of the " Two Regions," into which the land of Mizraim must always be divided—the broad flat alluvial plain of the Delta stretching out on every side further than the eye can reach, and the comparatively narrow valley of the Nile opening into it, bounded on either side by steep ranges of rocky hills, with the wide river running between them. The early Egyptians called the site " the Balance of the Two Regions;" and such it was most truly—it commanded both, it gave ready access to both, it joined both in a happy union from which each alike derived advantage. The excellency of the situation is sufficiently indicated by the fact, that though special causes—peculiar political conjunctures or ethnic leanings—may for a time draw away the seat of government to some other quarter, as to Thebes or Alexandria, yet it will always of necessity revert, after a longer or a shorter interval, to the old position—the site or near neighbourhood of the old capital. Cairo stands within a few miles of the spot on which Memphis formerly stood, and is to be viewed as representing it, and as continuing its ancient glories.

Striking natural beauty does not characterise any Egyptian site. " The landscape lacks the charm of form—the majesty of the Alps, the solemn line of Atlas, the asperity of the Lycian crags which tower above the Gulf of Adalia, the solid mass of snow-clad Lebanon, the pastoral softness of the Galilean hills. Plain and highland, meadow and forest, do not succeed one another, as in those varied lands which are each a little world complete in itself." [1] The scenery about Memphis is naturally monotonous and unexciting. Its main constituents are a broad, grey, more or less turbid river—a flat strip of land on either side, green, or yellow, or brown, according to the time of year, and two unimpressive ranges of low level hills, shutting in the view east and west within the distance of a few miles. Whatever beauty there is arises either from colouring or from the richness of the vegetation. Everywhere over the alluvial plain, as soon as the waters of the inundation have subsided, a rich growth springs up. Either there is a carpet of the greenest grass embroidered with flowers of a thousand varied

---

[1] See Mr. R. Stuart Poole's " Cities of Egypt," p. 1.

hues, or wheat and barley, and lupins, and flax, and clover cover the ground with a promise, which they soon keep, of a luxuriant harvest. Abundant acacias, mulberries, and sycamores shade the river banks, while among them occasionally shoots up the tall feathery palm, which has been well called " the queen of trees." In the gardens are now seen frequent groves of lemon and orange trees, which have replaced the " vines and fig-trees" (Ps. cv. 33) of ancient times. Over these and the distant hills and the buildings—mostly commonplace enough—the sun, shining ever in an unclouded sky, sheds the glamour of a magic light, which lends a marvellous beauty even to the most homely features of the scene, and spreads over the entire landscape a witchery which no pen can describe.

The existing remains of Memphis give no indication of its former greatness. Of the grand temple of Phthah, the most ancient and in some respects the most venerable shrine in Egypt, scarcely any vestiges remain beyond a few shapeless heaps, and one fallen colossus of Rameses II., which, when perfect, must have been nearly forty-five feet in height. As Ezekiel prophesied, "the idols have been destroyed, and the images made to cease out of Noph" (Ezek. xxx. 13), which presents now a picture of desolation. Most of the materials whereof the town was built have been carted away to Cairo, where almost every palace and mosque and tower is composed mainly of stones and marbles quarried by the early or the later Pharaohs to adorn their principal capital.

But one adjunct of Memphis, thoroughly characteristic of the ancient town, and always regarded as constituting one of its principal glories, still remains, a sufficient evidence of ancient grandeur and importance, viz., the Necropolis or "City of the Dead," which occupies the edge of the desert on the west of the city, stretching north and south nearly twenty miles, and containing thousands upon thousands of sepulchres. Here, among more than sixty others, are the "Three Great Pyramids," the tombs of Khufu, Shafra, and Menkanra, Pharaohs who lived before the time of Abraham, and on whose monuments his eyes probably often rested. Here is the Serapeum or subterranean gallery in which were buried, each in his own stone sarcophagus, and each in his own arched niche, the Sacred Bulls, worshipped during their lifetimes as "Hapi" or "Apis," and regarded as incarnations of Phthah. Here were miles upon miles of tombs ranged in streets, belonging to all orders and conditions of men and women, some of them massively built of stone, others cut in the sides of the rock, others again mere pits leading to chambers of sepulture. No such necropolis as this exists elsewhere in the entire world, no such accumulation of graves, not at Erech, the Babylonian " City of the Dead," not in the catacombs of Rome, not at Kerbela or at Meshed-Ali, the tomb cities of the Mahometans.

Such is Memphis as existing at the present day. The living town has disappeared, or is only to be seen in its representative, the modern Cairo; but the dead town is there stretched out for twenty miles, west and north-west and south-west of the ancient site, a wonderful memento of the times that are gone, more impressive in its multitudinousness and in its hoar antiquity than any collection of pillared fanes, or crumbling towers, or ruined palaces, such as show to the inquiring traveller where other capitals have stood.

Second to Memphis among the cities of Egypt in historical importance, but in magnificence and picturesqueness far transcending Memphis, was the other great Egyptian capital, the Metropolis of the South, Thebes. The vision of the Hebrew prophets and historians saw her dimly and indistinctly as a far-off city, heard of rather than visited, known to them as mighty and strongly fortified and "populous" (Nahum iii. 8), but beyond the sphere of their activity and but rarely attracting their attention (Jer. xlvi. 25; Ezek. xxx. 14-16). Their name for Thebes was "No" or "No-Amon," in which latter form we have the exact equivalent of the native "Nu-Amen" or "City of Ammon," which was the sacred name of the place. "No" probably represented "Nu-aa," "the Great City," which was another native designation, and the one from which the Assyrians formed their name of "Nia."

The situation of Thebes, though less suitable as a seat of government for the whole of Egypt than that of Memphis, was not without special advantages. The Nile valley at this point broadens out into a magnificent plain, at least ten miles in width, through which the great river flows, expanded by islands, and offering to the eye long reaches of rushing water. The plain is enclosed by an amphitheatre of hills. Towards the east the Arabian range recedes to the distance of seven or eight miles, while on the west the Libyan hills, after almost touching the river, retire, leaving a narrower semicircle. These hills, moreover, in this place, changing their usual character of a "desert-wall," straight and even at the top, rise in a peak-like form to the unusual height of twelve hundred feet, and in one place fall to the plain in a sheer scarped cliff.[1] The broad green plain on either side the river is an alluvium of the richest description; under cultivation it bears the most

[1] See Mr. R. Stuart Poole's "Cities of Egypt," p. 49.

I

abundant crops; and it is dotted over with *dom* and date palms, sometimes growing single, sometimes collected into clumps or groves. Here, too, there open out on either side, to the east and to the west, lines of route offering great advantages for trade—on the one hand with the Lesser Oasis, and so with the tribes of the African interior; on the other with the western coast of the Red Sea and the spice regions of the opposite shore. In the valley of Hammamât, down which passed the ancient route to the coast, are abundant supplies of *breccia verde*, and of other valuable and rare kinds of stone; while at no great distance to the right and left of the route lie mines of gold, silver, and lead, anciently prolific, though exhausted now for many ages. Somewhat more remote, yet readily accessible by a frequented route, was the emerald region of Gebel Zabara, where the mines are still worked,[1] though not at present very productive.

The ancient city was built chiefly on the eastern side of the river. Here were the two

---

[1] Wilkinson, "Topography of Thebes," p. 420.

great palace-temples known to moderns as those of Luxor and Karnak, at once the residences of the kings and the places of worship for both king and people—the most glorious and magnificent of all the buildings of antiquity. Here was the "Hall of Columns," erected by Seti I.—a single chamber, supported by a hundred and sixty-four massive stone pillars, and covering a larger area than the Cathedral of Cologne. Here were the lofty obelisks of Thothmes III. and Rameses II.; here were numerous colossi of these and other Pharaohs; here were the long avenues of human-headed and ram-headed sphinxes which connected the palace-temples with each other and with the river; here, lastly, were the residences of the mighty "multitude" whereby the town was peopled (Jer. xlvi. 25; Ezek. xxx. 15), and the walls and gates of which Homer sang to his contemporaries.[1] Towards the west, between the river and the Libyan range were only isolated temples and colossi—the temples of Rameses III. and of Hatasu at Medinet-Abou, the Ramesseum at

---

[1] *Iliad*, ix. 503.

Qurnah, the great colossi of Amenhotep III.
half-way between the mountains and the river,
and a few other unimportant edifices. The
right bank was the bank of the living, the left
bank the bank of the dead ; and at Thebes,
as at Memphis, there lay along the Libyan
range a necropolis, with the difference, however, that at Memphis the tombs attracted the
eye, while at Thebes they were chambers in
the rock, which sought, as far as was possible,
to avoid notice.

The palmy period of Thebes was the latter
part of the early Egyptian empire and the
early part of the third or latest empire. It
owed its principal glories to those Pharaohs
who are thought to have been the great
oppressors of the Israelites, Seti I. and his
son Rameses II. From the time of David
to the end of the independent kingdom the
city was of little account. In the eighth and
seventh centuries before our era it was repeatedly taken and sacked, sometimes by the
Ethiopians, sometimes by the Assyrians. The
prophet Nahum paints in vivid colours one
of these sieges, probably that conducted by

Asshur-bani-pal in B.C. 667 : "Art thou better than populous No, or No-Amon," he says, addressing Nineveh, "that was enthroned among the Nile streams, with the waters round about her, whose rampart was the deep, and her wall from the deep? Ethiopia and Egypt were her strength, and it was infinite; Phut and Lubim were thy helpers. Yet was she carried away, she went into captivity : her young children also were dashed in pieces at the top of all the streets ; and they cast lots for her honourable men, and all her great men were bound with chains " (chap. iii. 8–10). Thebes still bears the scars of this overthrow, from which she at no time fully recovered. Later kings, the Psamatiks and others, repaired in some measure her shattered edifices; but none succeeded in obliterating the traces of the Assyrian vengeance. Tottering columns, overthrown colossi, obelisks prone in the dust, give indications of a wanton destruction and disfigurement which may be best assigned to this time.

The walls and gate-towers of Thebes, like those of Babylon, have been completely de-

stroyed. They were probably of crude brick,
and having been defended externally by deep
moats, have gradually sunk and disappeared
in the receptacle placed so conveniently to
receive them. The gates, if they were of
bronze, as Homer declares, would naturally
have been carried off by the conquerors. The
houses of the common people, and even those
of the better class—all, in fact, but the
palaces of the kings—have crumbled down
to dust, and been made level with the plain
by the constant action of the annual inundation.

Migdol and Syene mark, in the phraseology
of the Hebrew prophets, the extreme limits of
Egypt towards the north and towards the
south (Ezek. xxix. 10, xxx. 6). Migdol is a
Semitic word, and means simply "a tower"
or "fort," so that it is not improbable that
there may have been several Migdols in Egypt.
One place of the name is well known. There
was, on the eastern frontier, about ten miles
south of Pelusium, a fortified place, which the
Greeks and Romans called "Magdôlus,"[1] and

---

[1] Hecat. Fr. 282 ; Itin. Antonin., p. 171, 3.

which we may assume that the Semites would have called " Migdol " and the Egyptians " Maktal." This is probably the " Migdol " of Jeremiah (chap. xliv. 1, xlvi. 14). It is conjecturally placed at Tel-es-Samoot, or at Tel-el-Hir, two mounds to the east of the Suez Canal, not far from Tineh, the admitted site of Pelusium. Another Migdol is located about midway in the isthmus, and is thought to have given name to the modern " Bir-Makdal." [1] A third is believed to have been situated near the modern Suez, and to be represented by the still existing " Muktala." [2] This last is perhaps the Migdol of Exodus (chap. xiv. 2) and Numbers (chap. xxxiii. 7). If the Migdol which is mentioned as the northern limit of Egypt must necessarily be regarded as one or other of these three, undoubtedly the preference must be given to the Migdol near Pelusium, alike as the most northern and as the most celebrated.

But it may be open to question whether there was not a fourth Migdol. The most

[1] See Dr Trumbull's " Kadesh Barnea," p. 375.
[2] Ibid.

northern point of Egypt was near the Seben-
nytic mouth of the Nile, in long. 31° 5′ nearly.
A fort or watch-tower is sure to have existed
at this spot, to keep an outlook upon naval
enemies and pirates. May not this fort have
been known as a Maktal or Migdol, and may
it not be the place intended by Ezekiel? If
these views are thought to be too purely
speculative, we must fall back on the Pelusiac
Migdol, which was perhaps sufficiently near
the northern frontier to be used in ordinary
speech as a synonym for the extreme north of
the country.

The site of this Migdol, whether we place
it at Tel-el-Hir or at Tel-es-Samoot, is in a
wretched district, half marsh, half sand. The
overflow of Lake Menzaleh is always spreading
further and further eastward, while the drift-
sand from the desert is always creeping further
and further westward. But this may have
been different in early times. Maktal was on
the high road by which the Egyptian armies
marched from Memphis to the invasion of
Asia. In ancient times it was no doubt well
guarded from floods by embankments, well

supplied by a canal with Nile water, and well protected in some way or other from the encroachment of the sand. Wherever the Nile water can be carried, human labour can create a garden, and Migdol may, under the great Pharaohs, have been as well provided with gardens and orchards and fruitful fields as Zoan. Still it was certainly at all times on the edge of the desert; and while westward it may have looked upon green fields and well-laden fruit-trees, eastward it must have confronted the awful sterility of the wilderness. Its most conspicuous feature was doubtless the tall watch-tower, from which an outlook was continually kept over the distant sandy plain, that would-be invaders might be descried from afar, and met on the frontier with force sufficient to drive them back.

Syene, which passed for the southern limit of Egypt in the ordinary popular parlance, offered a strong contrast to the Migdol which we have been describing. It was a quiet town on the right bank of the Nile, sheltered under the Arabian range of hills, and chiefly famous for its quarries, which furnished the best materials for building purposes, and especially for obelisks, to be found within the limits of the Egyptian territory. Between Silsilis and Syene the rock formation of Egypt changes its character, and from secondary sandstone and limestone becomes " primary," consisting of rose-coloured granite, syenite, and other kindred substances. The quarries of Syene were worked from a date anterior to Abraham, and supplied to all the most ambitious of the Temple-building Kings a material unequalled for durability and beauty, whereof they made a copious use. Hence Apepi, the contemporary of Joseph, obtained his blocks for the great fane of Set or Sutech at Zoan (Tanis) ; hence Osirtasen derived his Helipolitan obelisks ; hence the Pyramid - Kings procured their granite portcullises and sarcophagi ; hence the Thothmeses and Amenhoteps, the Setis and the Rameseses, obtained the main materials for their colossi, their obelisks, their Apis-tombs, and the like. Even now, in the still-existing quarries behind the town, may be seen an unfinished obelisk of pink granite, lying on its

side, half-hewn, as though awaiting comple-
tion.

The neighbourhood of Syene is striking, and
in many respects beautiful. The granite rocks
on either side of the river rise up precipitously
from the strip of plain at their base, and show
a strongly indented outline against the deep
azure of the cloudless sky. The river is
studded with islands, sometimes bare masses
of stone, sometimes covered with the thick
foliage of trees. Directly opposite to Syene,
on a large island lying midway in the course
of the stream, is Elephantine, one of the great
priestly towns, whose ruins are embosomed in
the greenest verdure, and bright with numerous flowers. About three miles above the
site of the town occurs the natural barrier,
which makes it reasonable to draw the line
between Egypt and Ethiopia at about this
point. This barrier is a ridge of rose-coloured
granite, which here crosses the channel of
the river, blocking up its course, and acting
during low Nile as a dam, which retains the
water of the upper stream at an elevation

of at least eighty feet above the level of the lower river. Where the ridge crosses the channel it is broken into a score or more of separate islets, which thrust up their jagged points above the surface, and greatly impede the navigation. Among these murderous reefs the waters of the First Cataract boil and surge, sometimes merely hurrying on at a mad pace, and forming what are called "rapids," sometimes becoming veritable "falls," a chaos of blinding foam and spray. But the great accession of water at the time of the inundation, submerging the rocks, substitutes for the Cataract of the dry season a mere rapid slope of stream, which the force of steam is able to overcome, and with which even the Nile boatmen cope successfully. Still the barrier is felt as a division set by Nature herself between the upper and lower countries, a division which man does well to note and follow. As Syene was reckoned the last Egyptian town towards the south by the Hebrews and the ancient Egyptians themselves, so was Philæ, in the still waters above the Cataract, regarded as the frontier city by the Romans ; while the modern tendency is to revert to the ancient demarcation line, and to make Assouan, which stands upon the site of Syene, once more the boundary.

THE END.

www.ingramcontent.com/pod-product-compliance
Lightning Source LLC
Chambersburg PA
CBHW070733030726
47601CB00001B/4